ROME

in your pocket

MAIN CONTRIBUTOR: JACK ALTMAN

PHOTOGRAPH CREDITS

The Travel Library front cover, 41; The Travel Library/A Amstel 57, 66, 82, 88; The Travel Library/Stuart Black back cover, title page, 9, 12, 13, 20, 26, 29, 31, 38, 39, 42, 44, 47, 48, 49, 50, 51, 52, 54, 67, 68, 70, 72, 78, 79, 84, 86, 87, 91, 93, 95 (right, left), 97, 98, 103, 106, 109, 111, 113, 117, 118, 121, 123; The Travel Library/Philip Enticknap 5, 7, 19, 23, 33, 35, 36, 55, 56, 65, 74, 75, 76, 101, 104, 105, 126; The Travel Library/Richard Glover 14, 63; The Travel Library/John Heseltine 73; The Travel Library/Peter Terry 43, 45; The Bridgeman Art Library 10, 25 (top, bottom), 58, 59, 61, 80; British Film Institute 17.

Front cover: The Colosseum; back cover: view of St Peter's; title page: statue of angel on Pont Sant'Angelo.

MANUFACTURE FRANÇAISE DES PNEUMATIQUES MICHELIN

Place des Carmes-Déchaux – 63000 Clermont-Ferrand (France)

© Michelin et Cie. Propriétaires-Éditeurs 1996

Dépôt légal Avril 97 – ISBN 2-06-650601-X – ISSN 1272-1689

Printed in Spain 10-98/3

MICHELIN TYRE PLC
Tourism Department
The Edward Hyde Building
38 Clarendon Road
WATFORD Herts WD1 1SX - UK
☎ (01923) 415000

MICHELIN TRAVEL PUBLICATIONS
Editorial Department
One Parkway South
GREENVILLE, SC 29615
☎ 1-800 423-0485

CONTENTS

INTRODUCTION

Visitors to Rome *know* they are in an eternal city. All its ages are present together. Every 21 April, the Romans celebrate with bells, brass bands, movies and fireworks the birth of their city in 753 BC. The centre of festivities is Michelangelo's Campidoglio where today's town hall, in a Renaissance palazzo, stands on the site of the ancient Roman Capitol. In Piazza Navona, fashionable Romans sit around Bernini's grand 17C Fountain of the Four Rivers on a square overlying the elongated oval of Emperor Domitian's sports stadium of AD 86. Fiats and Ferraris roar out of town along ancient thoroughfares still named Via Appia, Via Flaminia, and Via Aurelia.

The spiritual life is, of course, an integral part of the city's eternity. The Vatican, with its St Peter's Basilica and Sistine Chapel, elevate to the sublime the splendour of the Roman Empire that they succeeded. Baroque churches rise on the remains of ancient monuments. Caravaggio's paintings in Santa Maria del Popolo or San Luigi dei Francesi build a bridge between the sacred path of the saints and the everyday life of the people.

And the cheerfully pagan is also omnipresent. A whiff of aromatic herbs wafts among the young people on the Spanish Steps. On nearby Via Condotti, their well-heeled elders explore the city's most elegant boutiques or meet lovers at the Caffè Greco. The Baths of Caracalla, which once witnessed the legendary excesses of the fratricide emperor who built them, are now loud with the tamer excesses of opera; while rock and jazz fans head, like the ancients, for the beach resorts of Ostia and Fregene.

One of Rome's romantic sights, the Trevi Fountain, shows Ocean flanked by Abundance and Salubrity.

HOW TO USE THIS GUIDE

This guide is divided into four main sections:

A Swiss Guard on duty outside the Vatican gates.

Background sets the scene, beginning with the city's geography, and exploring its long, rich history, the people and their culture, empire-builders, churchmen, sinners, artists and film-makers. There is a special feature on Renaissance Art and Architecture.

Exploring Rome opens with a list of the top ten sights any visitor to Rome should try to see. Introducing Rome is a first walk to get your bearings around the city centre. There are then four detailed sections covering the sights and attractions in Ancient Rome, The Vatican and the Historic Centre, north and south. The guide then picks out five key museums and five churches to visit. The Walks around Rome section is designed to help you discover some of the city's less famous gems, and is followed by suggestions for excursions from Rome. The section is rounded off with a Gazetteer of the city's other sights and attractions.

Enjoying Your Visit provides friendly, no-nonsense advice on the day-to-day holiday activities which can make the difference between a good holiday and a great one – festivals and events, eating out, shopping, entertainment and nightlife, and sports.

A–Z Factfinder is an easy-to-use reference section packed with useful information, covering everything you may need to know on your visit, from tipping to transport, and from using the telephone to tourist information offices. A word of warning: opening hours and telephone numbers change all the time, so be sure to check first.

GEOGRAPHY

Rome's position marked it out for greatness. Halfway down the Italian peninsula, at the heart of the Mediterranean, it was founded on the Tiber river close to the coast, to command good port facilities, but far enough inland to escape easy conquest. The coastal plain and valleys through the Appennines enabled it to build for its armies and merchants the roads that created the power and wealth of its empire.

It is difficult today to make out Rome's historic seven hills. Centuries of building and earthquake subsidence have smoothed out the steeper slopes, making most of them more humps than hills, none much more than 50m (164ft) above sea level. East of a bend in the Tiber river is the Capitoline hill, marked by the Piazza Campidoglio. It is flanked to the south by the Palatine, where the legendary Romulus is said to have founded the city, and below which the Forum was laid out. To the north is the Quirinal where Italy's president has his palace, not far from the Trevi Fountain. (Of the adjacent Viminal hill, nothing remains but the name.) To the east are the Esquiline plateau, distinguished by the Church of Santa Maria Maggiore, and the Celian hill with its Celimontana gardens. The most southerly of the historic hills is the Aventine, sacred in antiquity and today a delightful residential neighbourhood in its own right, separate from the general bustle. In fact, on the other side of the river, there are eighth and ninth hills, the Vatican and the park of the Janiculum.

Rising 396km (246 miles) away in the Appennine mountains of Tuscany, the Tiber river (Tevere) meanders through the city from north to south before curving towards the sea, 20km (12 miles) to the south-west. Its role in city life is not as central as that of the Arno in Florence or the Seine in Paris, but it was navigable for barge traffic until the end of the 19C. Embankments built in 1880 finally halted the frequent flooding from autumn rains and spring thaw, and it has never been known to dry up in summer. Of the Tiber's tributaries which once ran between the hills only the Aniene remains, on the north side of town. (Another, the Spinona, was transformed into the Cloaca Maxima in the 6C BC – the city's first and still operative sewer.)

St Peter's Basilica, seen here from the Tiber, is one of the great landmarks of Rome.

For your orientation, the city's principal landmarks are man-made rather than geographical: the Spanish Steps at the heart of the elegant shopping district; the Colosseum east of the ancient Forum; at the other end, the equally colossal but less aesthetically pleasing Vittoriano Monument on the vast Piazza Venezia; the obelisk of the Piazza del Popolo at the top of the busy Via del Corso. Across the river, the round tower of Castel Sant'Angelo opens up the vista to St Peter's and the Vatican; and for your train excursions, the architecturally acclaimed modern Stazione Termini is easily located on the east side of the city centre.

This bronze Estruscan sculpture from the 5-4C BC shows the she-wolf with Romulus and Remus.

HISTORY

As the Romans say, *Se non è vero, è ben trovato* – roughly: 'If it's not true, it's still a good story'. Legend, then, says the city was founded on the Palatine hill on 21 April

753 BC by Romulus. His mother, a vestal virgin ravished by the warrior god Mars, had abandoned the twins **Romulus** and **Remus** on the Tiber, which carried them to the foot of the Palatine where they were suckled by a she-wolf, now the city's emblem.

From Kingdom to Republic

In mundane fact, the left – east – bank at a bend in the Tiber had been settled since at least 1500 BC. **Bronze Age** cabin dwellings kept to the healthy high ground, notably the Capitoline, Palatine and Aventine hills, to avoid the malarial marshland down by the river. From the 8C BC, around the legendary foundation date, the hilltop hamlets came together as a city-kingdom.

From 616 BC, kings of **Etruscan** origin built the city's first ramparts, the Cloaca Maxima sewage system to drain the swamps – site of the later Forum – and the Circus Maximus for public entertainment. But the **Romans** threw out these foreign monarchs to set up a republic in 509 BC. For four centuries, patrician governors maintained a delicate balance with the people, the plebeians. The latter elected tribunes to defend their rights in courts of law and ensure the distribution of grain for bread.

After subduing surrounding tribes, Rome was itself invaded by the **Gauls** in 390 BC – despite a warning by the sacred geese in the Temple of Juno. The city rebuilt its defences and suppressed the remaining external threats. Conquest of the Italian peninsula and neighbouring Mediterranean lands brought wealth to the patricians, but not to the people of Rome. From 133 to 121 BC the Gracchus brothers, the people's tribunes, promoted agrarian reforms against corrupt

Statue of Julius Caesar, who was to be dictator for only a month before he was assassinated.

land-owners, and were both assassinated. Unrest and civil war led to the brief, enlightened dictatorship of **Julius Caesar**, in turn assassinated in 44 BC.

Empire

Caesar's adopted son outwitted rivals to become Rome's first emperor, **Augustus**, in 27 BC. The city's monuments reflected the new imperial grandeur, an ever vaster Forum, temples, theatres; a literature developed to sing its praises, Virgil's *Aeneid* and Livy's *History of Rome*.

In the century of Christ's crucifixion and the destruction of Jerusalem, Christian and Jewish slaves and refugees in Rome faced martyrdom and persecution. **Nero** blamed the burning of the city in AD 64 on Christian terrorists and ordered the execution of the apostles Peter and Paul as their ring-leaders. Other emperors left a more creative mark: **Vespasian**'s Colosseum, **Titus**'s triumphal arch, **Trajan**'s Column, **Domitian**'s stadium (Piazza Navona) and **Hadrian**'s Pantheon and his mausoleum, now Castel Sant'Angelo.

The 2C was the empire's Golden Age, with Rome's population exceeding 1 000 000 under the philosopher **Marcus Aurelius** (AD 161–180). His humanitarian policies improved life for the poor, made criminal law more lenient and de-brutalized gladiatorial contests, but did not extend to Christians, who were still persecuted as his empire's natural enemies.

Rome Christianized

Over-extended into Asia and Germanic Europe in the 3C, the empire began to disintegrate, with a succession of 25 emperors in 75 years. The Christians continued to defy persecution until **Constantine** (306–337) found it easier to join them than beat them. Before moving to Byzantium (Constantinople) in 330, he built several churches in Rome, including San Giovanni in Laterano, St Peter's Basilica and San Lorenzo fuori le Mura.

Wealth and talent abandoned the divided empire's western capital for the east and, from 410, successive waves of **barbarians** – Visigoths, Vandals and Ostrogoths – left Rome ruined and deserted. The population

The Column of Trajan is decorated with scenes depicting Trajan's campaigns in Dacia.

13

had shrunk to 50 000 when the Germanic **King Odoacer** deposed Rome's last emperor, **Romulus Augustulus**, in 476. But **Pope Leo I** (440–461), persuading the Huns not to invade Rome and the Vandals not to exterminate its citizens, put the papacy firmly on the European stage. By the year 800, the coronation in St Peter's of **Emperor Charlemagne** asserted papal authority – and launched a perennial power struggle between Church and State.

Meanwhile, Rome was again prey to foreign invasion – by the Arabs in 846, and

A magnificent view of St Peter's Square and Rome can be seen from the dome of St Peter's Basilica.

by Henry IV in 1084 – and to civil strife between papal and imperial supporters. In 1309, the pope moved to the safety of Avignon. The populist tribune **Cola di Rienzo** established a republic in 1347, crushed seven years later by aristocrats who plunged the city once more into bloody street battles.

Renaissance and Counter-Reformation

Returning to Rome in 1377, the papacy reasserted its power with an iron fist. With the popes' blessing, the Renaissance in arts and sciences in the 15C and 16C accompanied a glorious rebirth for the city. A symbol of Rome's new grandeur was the rebuilding of St Peter's basilica. **Nicholas V**, **Julius II** and **Leo X** invited Italy's greatest architects, sculptors and painters – among them Bramante, Michelangelo, and Raphael – to make Rome once again the centre of the western world.

The new luxury attracted the rapacity of **Emperor Charles V**'s armies, who plundered the city in 1527, and, more durably, the wrath of **Luther** and his Protestant Reformation. The **Jesuits** were founded in 1540 to spearhead the Counter-Reformation, which aimed to re-establish the dignity and moral authority of the Church. Rome's Jews were for the first time forced to live in a ghetto and Protestants fled north. The Holy Office stepped up its Inquisition against heretics, burning to death the philosopher **Giordano Bruno** in 1600 and forcing **Galileo** to retract his theories in 1633. The papal Index banned the pagan themes of Renaissance art in favour of the more explicitly Christian – but no less sensuous – motifs of 17C Baroque.

Towards National Unity

In the 18C the Habsburg empire's control of Italy – by now an assortment of states, duchies and provinces – eroded papal supremacy, and it was a much weakened Rome that French soldiers conquered in 1798. After **Napoleon**'s defeat in 1814, the principal French legacy was a sense of national identity, with Rome as Italy's capital.

Hostile to such liberal ideas, **Pope Pius IX** fled Rome when **Giuseppe Mazzini** proclaimed a republic there in 1848. The French defeated **Garibaldi**'s republican troops and restored the papacy as a French protectorate. Italian unification was achieved without Rome in 1862 and the new kingdom had to await Napoleon III's abdication before seizing the city in 1870. A year later, with the pope retreating from the Quirinal Palace to the Vatican, Rome was proclaimed capital of a united Italy.

Modern Times

In the nationalistic atmosphere of 1911, the gigantic monument to **King Vittorio Emanuele II** was inaugurated on Piazza Venezia as a symbol of Italian unity. Its bombastic spirit heralded Italy's participation in World War I and the Fascists' March on Rome in 1922. The king handed dictatorial powers to **Benito Mussolini**. The Lateran Treaty of 1929 made Catholicism the state religion, and, in exchange for the papacy's abandoning claims to the Papal States, recognized the Vatican as a sovereign state. Until he was toppled in 1943, Mussolini (*il Duce*) saw himself as successor to the Roman emperors, bulldozing monuments and whole neighbourhoods to make way for vast new thoroughfares and his own Mussolini Forum (now Foro Italico) sports complex.

Pope Pius XII, who as Cardinal Eugenio Pacelli had negotiated the concordat with Nazi Germany in 1933, was criticized for staying silent about the Nazi persecution of Jews and not trying to save 2 000 Jews deported during the German occupation of Rome in 1943. Liberated in 1944, Rome itself was declared an open city and largely spared from bombing.

After the war, Italy had its own 'economic miracle', celebrated in the 1960s with *la dolce vita* in the cafés and nightclubs of the Via Veneto and encapsulated in Fellini's film *La Dolce Vita*. In the 1970s, the city was hit with bombs and kidnappings by Red Brigade and Neo-Fascist terrorists. The Mafia moved in to

Anita Ekberg and Marcello Mastroianni in the famous Trevi Fountain scene from Fellini's La Dolce Vita.

manipulate power in the government and launder money in the Vatican's banks, belatedly countered by crusading magistrates. The media magnate **Silvio Berlusconi** also came to town as prime minister, but found Rome's political waters difficult to navigate. Power-mongers may come and go, but what matters most to modern Romans – as it did to their ancestors when chariots bustled around the ancient Forum – is how to handle the downtown traffic.

Café scene in Piazza Navona, one of Rome's most beautiful Baroque squares.

THE PEOPLE AND THE CULTURE

Rome is the national capital and its citizens have the self-assurance that stems from such pre-eminence. Sophisticated, hard-working Milanese, for instance, dismiss the infuriatingly easy-going Romans as 'provincials'. Certainly, in a nation so theatrical and demonstrative, Romans often resist any show of emotion and avoid expansive gestures. More relaxed than northerners, less excitable than Neapolitans, they cultivate instead a studied indifference – known as *menefreghismo*. But this is only the Romans' own equally theatrical way of proclaiming their coolness. Notice how, responding to an irate tourist with scarcely more than a raised eyebrow, a waiter may look to his colleagues after the storm has passed for some silent applause for his splendid imperturbability.

In a town where, besides tourism, the main occupations are government and the Church, Romans are masters of the *combinazione* needed to get a job, an apartment, a permanent parking-space or even a cemetery place, through a well-placed friend. In the cafés, the wheelers and

A group of nuns enjoying the sights of Rome.

dealers are not so discreet: regognition of their ability to get a thing done is communicated with a hand ostentatiously cupped around the mouth. And the clergy never lets you forget that this is the nerve-centre of Christianity, where nuns whizz around on motor scooters and cardinals pass the good word on mobile phones.

ART AND ARCHITECTURE

Very few great artists were born in Rome, but the city always acted as a magnet for the best talents. Typically, its **Etruscan** tomb sculpture and terracotta figures showed a heavy **Greek** influence but were imbued with a native sensuality, underlined in the bold colour of the tomb paintings. From the

4C BC, sculptors modified the Hellenistic style with the Roman taste for monumental realism. This became more pronounced as imperial art emphasized the official virtues of state service over and above the aesthetic idealization and harmony of the Greeks.

In architecture, Rome's traditional pragmatism was expressed in the efficient use of building materials. Where Greeks used marble and granite for an angular architecture of columns and plinths, Rome turned more to bricks and concrete (first adopted for mass production in the 2C BC) for the rounded forms of arches, vaults and domes. Walls became more important than columns. All these elements are apparent in the Colosseum, Hadrian's Pantheon, the Baths of Caracalla and Constantine's Triumphal Arch.

With interior columns enclosed by external walls, the Roman basilica turned the Greek temple inside out. This can be still be seen, beneath heavy Baroque overlay, in the church of Santa Maria Maggiore, built in the 5C in classical Roman style. The nave still has its 5C Byzantine mosaics over the triumphal arch.

Between the 14C and the 16C came the tremendous outburst of creativity that we call the **Renaissance** (*see* p.24). Reaction followed when, in 1573, the Jesuit church of Il Gesù ushered in an initially austere expression of the new **Baroque** architecture. In painting, following **Mannerists** like Giulio Romano, Rosso Fiorentino and Pontormo, who were perceived as too aristocratic and even somewhat effete, leaders of the Church's Counter-Reformation wanted a strong, more assertive style to reaffirm the popular appeal of Catholicism. Caravaggio's pictures of *St Paul* and *St Peter* for Santa Maria del Popolo and *St Matthew* for San Luigi dei Francesi were rather more realistic than expected, but popular in appeal. The Carracci brothers' frescoes for the Palazzo Farnese were more pleasingly decorous.

Bernini and **Borromini** were the 17C Baroque's most brilliant architects and fiercest rivals. On Piazza Navona, Bernini's Fountain of the Four Rivers confronts Borromini's church of Sant'Agnese. They worked together on St Peter's. Bernini triumphed with his St Peter's Square and the basilica's great bronze canopy and pulpit, making his name above all as the age's supreme sculptor. Borromini achieved glory with his Palazzo Barberini and the churches of Sant'Ivo alla Sapienza and San Carlo alle Quattro Fontane.

The 18C gave Rome two of its most popular monuments – the Spanish Steps and the Trevi Fountain. It also saw, under the German Johann Joachim Winckelmann, the beginning of systematic scientific archaeology to excavate the ancient Roman past.

Detail of a figure representing the River Ganges, in Bernini's splendid Fountain of the Four Rivers, Piazza Navona.

Theatre, Opera and Cinema

Rome's theatrical inclinations took over in the 19C and 20C. **Rossini**'s opera *The Barber of Seville* had its première in 1816 – and flopped at first – but **Verdi**'s *Trovatore* and **Puccini**'s *Tosca* were huge successes. With his awareness of cinema's propaganda value, Mussolini made his one contribution to Italian culture in 1937, building the Cinecittà studios. **Roberto Rossellini** and **Sergio Leone** were both born in Rome, and **Vittorio de Sica**, **Federico Fellini** and **Pier Paolo Pasolini** lived there. Talents like **Nanni Moretti** may yet revive the noble art.

Renaissance Art and Architecture

This intellectual and cultural revolution had its roots in the humanist philosophy, the poetry and the painting of the Italian 14C. By the following century it reached great heights, with the new use of perspective and a new understanding of the human body based on scientific principles. Rome's pre-eminence made it a focus of artistic activity, and the patronage of successive popes was a major contributing factor. **Leon Battista Alberti**, hired in 1447 as consultant to Pope Nicholas V, made the bridge between ancient Roman and Renaissance architecture. The great humanist adapted the superimposed classical architectural orders of the Colosseum for the design of 15C churches and palaces.

At the same time, Alberti's fellow Florentine, **Fra Angelico**, was painting frescoes for the chapel of Nicholas V with a Roman grandeur quite unlike the delicate style of his painting back in Tuscany. By the 1480s, artists streamed into Rome to paint the first frescoes for the Sistine Chapel – **Botticelli**, **Ghirlandaio** and **Piero di Cosimo** from Florence, **Perugino**, **Pinturicchio** and **Signorelli** from Umbria.

By 1500, there was an absolute explosion of activity. **Donato Bramante**, pioneering master architect of the High Renaissance, was nicknamed *Bramante Ruinante* as he tore down ancient monuments to make way for the new. He was commissioned by Pope Julius II to rebuild St Peter's, producing a centrally planned church beneath a dome with coffered interior, one of the first such designs since antiquity. St Peter's was subsequently extended by a longitudinal nave, but Bramante's concept, beautifully realized, can be seen in his **tempietto** for San Pietro in Montorio (*see* p.85).

Michelangelo and Raphael

Meanwhile, Julius II had brought in **Michelangelo** in 1505 not only to create frescoes for the Sistine Chapel, but also to make

sculptures for the pope's monumental tomb, of which the *Moses* at San Pietro in Vincoli was just one gigantic part. **Raphael** was working in the Vatican on his grandiose frescoes for the Stanze (papal apartments). He had also succeeded Bramante, one of a dozen master architects working on St Peter's in the 16C, including Michelangelo **Antonio da Sangallo the Younger** and Michelangelo.

Detail showing Delphic Sibyl, from the Sistine Chapel ceiling.

La Fornarina (c.1516) by Raphael (Palazzo Barberini).

EXPLORING ROME

MUST SEE

For a first-time visitor to Rome, there is a wealth of things to see. Here are suggestions for ten sights you really would regret missing, arranged alphabetically.

Coloseo★★★ (Colosseum)

Celebrated symbol of the city's imperial might, a magnificent arena that satisfied bloodthirsty spectators with deadly gladiatorial combats.

The Colosseum is one of Rome's most famous sights – and quite rightly so, representing the skill of the ancient Romans as builders.

Pantheon★★★
The beautifully preserved domed interior
makes Hadrian's 2C temple the handsomest
of the city's ancient monuments.

Piazza del Popolo★★
The rich focus of Roman life, with
fashionable cafés, Santa Maria del Popolo's
Caravaggio paintings, and two Baroque
churches on the south side.

Piazza Navona★★★
On the elegant, elongated site of the ancient
Roman sports stadium, cafés, ice-cream
parlours and painters surround Bernini's
fountain and Borromini's church of
Sant'Agnese in Agone.

Foro Romano★★★ (Roman Forum)
Wander among pillars and triumphal arches
to imagine ancient downtown Rome with its
politicians, businessmen, priests – and
ordinary people shopping in the market.

Basilica di San Pietro★★★ (St Peter's Basilica)
Grandiose St Peter's Square proclaims the
majesty of Catholicism's most important
church. Inside, see Bernini's bronze canopy
over the high altar and Michelangelo's *Pietà*
and dome.

Scala della Trinità dei Monti★★★ (Spanish Steps)
The perennially popular meeting-place,
leading to Piazza di Spagna and Via dei
Condotti's romantic Caffè Greco.

Fontana di Trevi★★★ (Trevi Fountain)
This glorious 18C monument was where
Anita Ekberg waded in for *La Dolce Vita* (*see*

p.17) and where lovers toss in coins to ensure their return to Rome.

Musei Vaticani★★★ (Vatican Museums)

In addition to Michelangelo's Sistine Chapel frescoes, the papal art-collections include Egyptian and Greco-Roman treasures, Raphael's frescoes in the Stanze, Fra Angelico's in Nicholas V's chapel, and paintings by Giotto, Titian and Caravaggio.

View across the busy Piazza del Popolo to the Egyptian obelisk of Ramses II. This square was the site of many public executions in the 18C and 19C.

Villa Borghese★★

Refreshing garden greenery for picnics, with museums – **Galleria Borghese★★★**, **Villa Giulia's Etruscan art★★★** in a 17C palace, and the **Galleria d'Arte Moderna★** (Gallery of Modern Art).

INTRODUCING ROME

Begin your lavish banquet of sightseeing with a selection of *antipasti* for a varied taste of riches to come. Our walk into the city centre takes in a couple of piazzas, some churches, an ancient monument or two, shopping streets and good cafés, ending up at the Trevi Fountain. Saving museums for another time, this itinerary can easily be done in a day.

Piazza del Popolo★★

The bustling square at the city centre's north end has, since antiquity, marked the starting point of **Via Flaminia**, Rome's great road link to northern Italy. The monumental gateway, **Porta del Popolo**, is a 16C replacement of the ancient Porta Flaminia. The piazza's Egyptian **Obelisk** of Ramses II dates from 1232 BC and was brought to Rome by Emperor Augustus. The lions at the base are a 19C addition.

Adjoining the gateway, the church of
Santa Maria del Popolo★★ is so named
because the original edifice (1099) was paid
for not by the Church but from the funds of
the people's commune. The present 15C
church is a fine example of Renaissance
harmonies, with Bramante adding an apsidal
choir in 1505. Inside, see Caravaggio's
paintings★★★ (1601) in the **Cerasi chapel**,
the brutally dramatic *Conversion of St Paul*
and *Crucifixion of St Peter*. Between the two is
Annibale Carracci's more idealized *Assumption of the Virgin*. The **Chigi chapel** was built
by Raphael, who also designed the cupola's
mosaics. Bernini's sculptures are on either
side of the altar.

For your cappuccino, choose between the
equally fashionable but fiercely rival **Caffè
Rosati** and **Caffè Canova**. For a while, the
demise of ideology blurred lines between
the left-wing crowd frequenting Rosati and
the right-wing regulars at Canova, but old
allegiances are returning. The piazza is
neatly completed on its south side by Carlo
Rainaldi's twin 17C Baroque churches, **Santa
Maria di Montesanto** (to the west), **Santa
Maria dei Miracoli** (to the east).

Via del Corso
This is the central and busiest thoroughfare
of the 'trident' of streets stabbing south
from Piazza del Popolo. Carnival horse races
held here till the 19C have been replaced by
cars equally hell-bent on being the first to
reach Piazza Venezia. If the shops and
restaurants on the side streets are chic and
expensive, those directly on the raucous Via
del Corso are more moderately priced. As
soon as the traffic gets to be too much, turn
left (east) to the calm of boutiques and

The Via del Corso, where riderless horse races were held during Carnival, is nowadays full of shoppers, tourists and traffic.

antique dealers on **Via del Babuino**, and art galleries on tranquil **Via Margutta**. The film director Federico Fellini lived here until his death in 1993 – for many people, the greatest Italian artist of the 20C.

Piazza di Spagna★★★ (Spanish Square)
Taking its name from the Spanish Embassy originally located here, the piazza is pure theatre, a marvellous combination of refinement, harmony and disorder. Young and old, lovers and pickpockets, tourists and street-vendors wander or lounge against the backdrop of the 18C **Spanish Steps**★★★. The gracefully curving staircase climbs the Pincio hillside to the twin belfries of **Trinità dei Monti**★, a French church of the 16C. Immediately in front of the church is an ancient Roman imitation of an Egyptian

obelisk. Back down on the piazza, take a few minutes rest and enjoy a refreshing rest next to the **Barcaccia fountain★** (Fontana della Barcaccia, 1629). Representing a sinking ship, this fountain is a work for which scholars contest the credit between Bernini and his father – charming either way.

Overlooking the Steps at Piazza di Spagna 26 is the **Keats House** where the poet John Keats spent the last years of his life. A museum displays memorabilia of the poet and his romantic contemporaries, Shelley and Byron. Across the square and equally British is that incongruous Victorian institution, **Babington's Tea Rooms** (popular with Americans, too, as an alternative to the less quaint McDonald's on the other side of the steps).

Via Condotti, most elegant of Rome's shopping streets, leads away from the piazza to the **Caffè Greco**, with its lavish décor of gilded mirrors, brocade-covered walls and marble tables, founded at number 86 in 1760 by Niccolò della Maddalena, a Greek. Its illustrious customers have included Stendhal, Baudelaire, Byron, Hans Christian Andersen, Goethe, Wagner and Liszt.

Piazza and Palazzo Borghese

Largo della Fontanella di Borghese prolongs Via Condotti to lead you – after negotiating the treacherous traffic of Via del Corso – to a delightful open-air **antiques market**, selling mainly old prints and books. The piazza is dominated by the sprawling late-Renaissance **Palazzo Borghese**, known for its shape as the 'harpsichord' and now housing the Spanish Embassy. In the inner courtyard are splendid gardens designed by Carlo Rainaldi, with ornate fountains and statuary.

The Fontana della Barcaccia, with the Spanish Steps beyond.

Montecitorio (Parliament and Government)
On its T-shaped piazza, the 17C **Palazzo di
Montecitorio** houses Italy's tumultuous
Chamber of Deputies, its handsome convex
façade originally designed by Bernini for the
more decorous papal courts of justice. The
gigantic early 20C rear section is lightened
by Art Nouveau designs, called in Italian *stile
Liberty*, after the London department store's
ornate fabrics. The prime minister's noble
Renaissance **Palazzo Chigi** is on the adjacent
Piazza Colonna. It looks out on the **Column
of Marcus Aurelius** (built between176-193),
which commemorates in bas-relief the
emperor's campaigns against Germanic
tribes along the Danube. In 1589, as part of
the Counter-Reformation, a statue of St Paul
replaced that of Marcus Aurelius on top of
the column.

Fontana di Trevi★★★ (Trevi Fountain)
Cross back over the Via del Corso to finish
your first day at the most romantic of Roman
fountains, its charm miraculously resisting
the assaults of 20C commercialization. Take
your first look now, but try to see it again in
peace at dawn or in the middle of the night.
Nicolà Salvi designed the basins, artificial
rocks and statues of the fountain in 1732, to
form part of a new colonnaded façade for
the Palazzo Poli with a triumphal arch at its
centre.

A giant figure of Ocean stands on a
cockleshell drawn by winged horses, one
bucking to the storm, the other quiet in still
waters, each guided by a triton. In the left-
hand niche, above an allegorical figure of
Abundance, a bas-relief shows General
Agrippa approving the design of the
aqueduct which brings the waters to the

The Trevi Fountain is one of Rome's most famous attractions.

fountain from the Acqua Vergine source at
Salone 20km (12 miles) east of Rome. The
bas-relief above the right-hand statue of
Salubrity depicts the young virgin who
showed the source to a band of Roman
soldiers.

For the coin-trick to work, guaranteeing
your return trip to Rome, throw the coin

*Ocean is the central
figure of the Trevi
Fountain, on his
cockleshell chariot
drawn by winged
horses.*

over your shoulder with your back to the
fountain. Long before (and since) Fellini
sent Anita Ekberg and Marcello Mastroianni
splashing in, street-kids have been wading
into the water to gather up the coins before
they are collected for the municipal budget.

ANCIENT ROME

Most of the principal monuments of Roman
antiquity are in and around the Roman
Forum and Colosseum. Some, like the
Pantheon, are best visited on a tour of the
Historic Centre (see p.64). The rest are in
the **Gazetteer** (see p.91).

Before visiting the Roman Forum, take a
first look at the whole area from **Capitoline
Hill** (Campidoglio), north-west of the
excavated site. The best observation point is
behind the city hall (Palazzo Senatorio) at
the back of Piazza del Campidoglio (see p.64).
Right of the palazzo, Via del Campidoglio
leads to a terrace directly overlooking the
Forum. From here, you can get a good
overview of the layout, and with the help of
a guide book you can work out your route.

Foro Romano★★★ (Roman Forum)

Stand amid fragments of architraves,
pediments and pedestals, columns, upright
or fallen, and imagine that people began
meeting here 2 600 years ago to shop,
gossip, govern, hatch plots, worship their
gods and bury their dead. It is a miracle
anything remains from this heart of an
ambitious republic and mighty empire.
Barbarians plundered and wrecked basilicas,
temples and triumphal arches in the 5C and
6C AD. Renaissance popes and princes
carried off marble and granite for their
churches and palaces. In the Counter-

Reformation, Baroque churches were defiantly built amid the pagan ruins, often from recycled ancient masonry. Serious archaeological excavation began only in 1803.

On the Forum's north side, the main entrance halfway along Via dei Fori Imperiali passes between scant remains of the **Basilica Aemilia**, a business and banking centre, and, to the left, temple columns incorporated in the 11C church of **San Lorenzo in Miranda** – its Baroque façade was added in 1602.

Beyond the basilica is a modern restoration of Diocletian's brick-built **Curia★★** or Senate House (AD 283).

The Forum was the centre of the political, social and judicial activities of Ancient Rome.

The Arch of Septimius Severus is one of the best preserved monuments in the Forum.

The most prominent monument at the Forum's west end is the **Arco di Settimio Severo★★** (Arch of Septimius Severus) (AD 203). Bas-reliefs celebrate triumphs by the emperor and his sons, Caracalla and Geta. Despite their father's deathbed injunction to live in peace, Caracalla killed his brother and erased his name from the arch. Nearby are traces of the **Rostra★** platform from which Mark Antony is believed to have made his funeral oration for Julius Caesar.

Three Corinthian columns form the corner of the **Tempio di Vespasiano★★** (Temple of Vespasian) (AD 81), diagonally across from the eight columns and architrave (5C AD) of the **Tempio di Saturno★★★** (Temple of Saturn), founded 900 years earlier to protect the state treasury.

Leading east to the Colosseum is the Forum's main street, **Via Sacra**, where victorious generals paraded prisoners, wagons laden with spoils of war, and proud legions. To the right of it is the **Colonna di Foca★** (Column of Phocas), a Corinthian

Colosseo*** (Colosseum)

As an emblem, the **Colosseum***** certainly evokes the awesome reality of the Roman Empire. It was started by Emperor Vespasian in AD 72, and the building was inaugurated eight years later by his son, Titus. The dimensions of the ellipse are: 188m (617ft) long, 156m (512ft) wide, 57m (187ft) high, with a capacity crowd of over 50 000. It replaced an artificial lake serving the Domus Aurea palace of Nero (under-going restoration) whose long-gone colossal statue gave the stadium its name in the Middle Ages.

Beasts and gladiators

A Roman historian wrote that 5 000 wild beasts were killed at one of the Colosseum's first spectacles – bears, lions, panthers, leopards and elephants. Gladiators fought for their freedom as prisoners of war, slaves or common-law criminals, occasionally for glory. The last show at the Colosseum was in 523, though man-to-man contests were halted a century before in favour of animal slaughter only.

Contrary to the legend, there is no historical evidence that Christians were 'fed to the lions' or otherwise killed for their religious beliefs at the Colosseum.

The architecture

Renaissance builders used as a school-book model the façade's superimposed Doric,

Ionic and Corinthian half-columned arcades. The pilastered wall at the top supported a canopy for shade. Inside, earthquakes and centuries of quarrying stone for churches and palaces have stripped the stadium to its brilliantly conceived skeleton. That intricate system of 80 entrances, radial ramps and stairways, passages and ambulatories to get thousands of spectators in and out fast leaves no doubt that this was an efficient empire. The wooden flooring has gone, revealing corridors and underground quarters of the gladiators and wild beasts.

Inside the Colosseum.

Planning a route around the site at the Forum.

pillar brought here from another monument in 608 to honour the Byzantine Emperor Phocas for donating the Pantheon (*see* p.78) to the Catholic Church. To the right, behind pedestals for the Via Sacra's honorary columns, are the remains of Julius Caesar's **Basilica Julia★★**, which enclosed four law courts. East of the basilica, three Corinthian columns remain from the

Tempio di Castore e Polluce★★★ (Temple of Castor and Pollux), built to celebrate the twins' divine intervention at a Roman victory over the Etruscans in 484 BC.

In AD 141, the Emperor Antoninus Pius built the **Tempio di Antonino e Faustina**★★ (Temple of Antoninus and Faustina) on the death of his wife, Faustina. When Antoninus himself died in AD 161 the temple was rededicated to them both. In the 11C the church of San Lorenzo in Miranda was built in the ruins, because it was thought that San Lorenzo (St Lawrence) had been condemned to death on the site. The church was rebuilt in the 17C, and is a strange sight

The portico of the Temple of Antoninus and Faustina (AD 2C) enclosing the Baroque façade of the church of San Lorenzo in Miranda.

today as the Baroque façade rises behind the Roman columns of the original temple.

Part of the circular **Tempio delle Vestale★★★** (Temple of Vesta) survives as a curved stone wall behind three of a ring of 20 columns. Rebuilt around AD 193 and dedicated to the goddess of fire, it recalls the round hut in which the communal fire was protected at the dawn of Rome's existence.

The six Vestal Virgins, whose job it was to look after the fire, lived in the rectangular building next door, the **Atrio delle Vestale** (House of the Vestal Virgins). Starting between the ages of six and ten and remaining virgins for the 30 years of their service, they were chosen – and punished for infractions such as letting the fire out or strange men in – by the *pontifex maximus*, a title inherited by the pope. In recognition of their service, statues of the senior Vestals were erected in the gardens of the House,

The statues of important Virgins in the remains of the gardens of the House of the Vestal Virgins.

Right: The lovely Temple of Vesta was one of the most elegant buildings on the Forum, with its fine fluted columns and circular shape reflecting the original wooden and thatched building which housed the eternal flame.

and this remains one of the most evocative and haunting parts of the Forum today.

Across Via Sacra is the concave façade of the **Tempio di Romolo** (Temple of Romulus) – not Rome's founder but the son of Emperor Maxentius – erected to honour the boy's death in AD 309. It retains its original bronze door and has been incorporated into the church of St Cosmas and St Damian since the 6C (*see* p.96). To the east, the gigantic **Basilica di Massenzio e Costantino★★★** (Basilica of Maxentius and Constantine), begun by Maxentius in the early 4C, and added to by Constantine, was conceived with brick and stone arches and vaulted halls closer in style to imperial baths than a traditional basilica. At the western end of what was the largest building in the Forum, was the equally massive statue of Constantine, standing 12m (39 ft) high. The remains of this can be seen in the courtyard of the Capitoline Museum (*see* p.67).

One of the more handsome churches inside the Roman Forum is the **Santa Francesca Romana** with its 17C Palladian façade and a Romanesque campanile of the 12C. The church's convent houses archaeological finds from the Roman Forum, including sarcophagi from the 9C BC.

At the Forum's south-eastern exit, the **Arco di Tito★★** (Arch of Titus) celebrates the Romans' destruction of Jerusalem in AD 70. The Jews had grown weary of being exploited by the Romans who ruled over them, and in AD 68 they rebelled. After two years of bitter fighting the Jews were finally defeated. The bas-reliefs on the interior of the arch represent the Emperor Titus's triumphal return to Rome with Jewish captives and booty from the Temple of

Jerusalem. The seven-branch *menorah* candelabra earned the monument the medieval name of **Arch of the Seven Lamps**.

Arco di Costantino★★★
(Arch of Constantine)

The composite but handsome arch honouring Constantine's victory over his rival Maxentius at the Milvian Bridge was erected in AD 315. At this battle north of Rome three years earlier, the new emperor is said to have seen a cross in the sky, bringing about his conversion to Christianity.

The impressive Arch of Constantine faces the Colosseum.

The reliefs on the inside of the arch depicting Trajan's victory of the Dacians were probably by the artist who worked on the Trajan's Column (*see* p.93-94).

Detail from the Arch of Constantine.

Terme di Caracalla★★★ (Baths of Caracalla)
After the death of his father Severus in York – and consolidating his own position by slaughtering his brother and 20 000 of his supporters – Caracalla made all free inhabitants of the empire Roman citizens. This was no act of magnanimity: the money he was then able to raise from taxes funded his grandiose building plans, of which the Baths of Caracalla are the most famous.

No mere public bath, Caracalla's 3C installation was the most opulent of spa resorts and health clubs, covering 27 acres

The sheer scale of the Baths of Caracalla cannot fail to impress.

Detail from a mosaic at the Baths of Caracalla.

(11 hectares) and serving some 1 600 people. Besides baths and two gymnasiums, it came with shops, libraries – one Greek, one Latin – conference rooms, sports stadium and gardens. (Some of the baths' splendid mosaic tiling and sculptures are displayed in the Vatican's museums.)

Two small entrance lobbies on either side led via dressing-rooms to a porticoed gymnasium, probably open-air, with adjoining *laconica* (saunas). The grand circular *caldarium* (hot bath) had a large central pool surrounded by six smaller ones; it is here that the summer opera festival is now staged (*see* p.107). In the middle of the building was the vaulted *tepidarium* to calm your heart-beat and, back at the entrance, the *frigidarium* (cold bath), probably an open-air swimming pool. The baths dried up in the 6C after Gothic invaders smashed the aqueduct supplying the water.

VATICANO★★★ (THE VATICAN)

The Vatican's 44 hectares (109 acres) make it the smallest state in the world. To avoid sightseeing overdose, visit St Peter's and the Vatican's palace and museums on separate days. The pilgrimage for faithful and sceptic alike starts at the Tiber river.

Ponte Sant'Angelo★

This bridge, built in AD 136 for Emperor Hadrian's mausoleum, has been 'Christianized' by 16C statues of the apostles Peter and Paul and Bernini's ten 'breezy maniac' angels. They owe the nickname to their wind-swept robes and the somewhat crazed way they brandish instruments of Christ's Passion – nails, crown of thorns and cross.

The Ponte Sant'Angelo, with its 16C statues, leads to the Castel Sant'Angelo.

Castel Sant'Angelo★★★

Map of the Vatican.

The massive imperial mausoleum, completed in AD 139 for Hadrian and his successors, was incorporated into the city's fortifications in the 3C. The **Passetto**, a high wall linking the castle to the Vatican Palace, was built in the 9C. The popes added bastions and made it a residential castle – and prison – for troubled times such as the sack of Rome in 1527. Thirty years earlier, a covered passageway to the Castel was built along the Passetto for quick escape from the Vatican.

The bronze **Sant'Angelo** – the Archangel Michael – replaced a statue depicting Hadrian as the sun-god Apollo driving a four-horse chariot. A spiral ramp leads past papal apartments and less opulent prison cells. See, too, the castle's collection of arms

There are sweeping views across Rome from the terrace of the Castel Sant'Angelo.

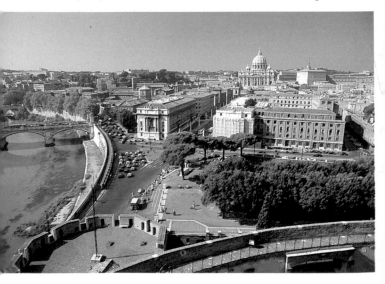

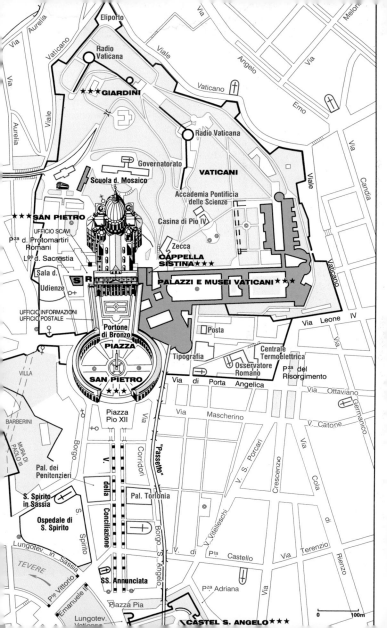

Eliporto

Via Aurelia

Viale Vaticano

Via Angelo

Via Melon

Via

Radio Vaticana

★★★ **GIARDINI**

Via Aurelia

Viale Aurelia

Radio Vaticana

Governatorato

Scuola d. Mosaico

VATICANI

Accademia Pontificia delle Scienze

★★★ **SAN PIETRO**

UFFICIO SCAVI

Casina di Pio IV

Pza d. Protomartiri Romani

Zecca

Lgo d. Sacrestia

CAPPELLA SISTINA ★★★

Sala d.

Udienze

PALAZZI E MUSEI VATICANI ★★★

UFFICIO INFORMAZIONI
UFFICIO POSTALE

Posta

Via Leone IV

Portone di Bronzo

Tipografia

Centrale Termoelettrica

PIAZZA

Osservatorio Romano

Pza del Risorgimento

SAN PIETRO
★★★

Via di Porta Angelica

Via Ottaviano

VILLA

Piazza Pio XII

Via Mascherino

V. Catone

BARBERINI

Borgo

Corridori

"Passetto"

V. S. Porcari

Crescenzio

Cola

MURA DI PAOLO III

V. della

Pal. dei Penitenzieri

Pal. Torlonia

di

S. Spirito in Sassia

Conciliazione

Borgo S. Angelo

V. Vitelleschi

Via Terenzio

Ospedale di S. Spirito

Via di Pta Castello

Via Rienzo

Lungotev. in Sassia

Spirito

SS. Annunciata

Pza Adriana

TEVERE

Pte Vittorio Emanuele II

Lungotev. Vaticano

Piazza Pia

0   100m

CASTEL S. ANGELO ★★★

The massive bronze statue of the Archangel Michael, by Pieter Verschaffelt, tops the Castel Sant'Angelo.

and armour and the wonderful roof-terrace **view★★★** over St Peter's and the historic centre (*see* pp.64-79).

Via della Conciliazione

Planned since the Renaissance, the processional street with obelisk lamp-posts marching solemnly west from the Tiber to St Peter's was inaugurated for the Holy Year of 1950. To make way for it, Mussolini began razing the Borgo neighbourhood's old houses in 1936.

Piazza San Pietro★★★ (St Peter's Square)
The piazza, designed for St Peter's Basilica
in 1656, is Bernini's most eloquent
masterpiece. This exuberant but devout
disciple of the Catholics explicitly conceived
the colonnade's grandiose oval as an
embracing welcome for all Christendom.
Pope Alexander VII wanted an atrium from
which the maximum number of faithful

*Crowds gather in St
Peter's Square for
the Papal Blessing.*

One of the many saints' statues outside St Peter's Basilica.

could see the pontiff on the balcony, or in his apartments on the north side of the square. Beneath statues of 140 saints, the rounded colonnade's four rows of columns are spaced for carriages and processions to pass under the covered gallery. The giant red granite **obelisk** was brought from Egypt by Caligula in AD 37 and hoisted here in 1587.

The Vatican Palace and Museums★★★

Frequent shuttle buses run from St Peter's Square to the Vatican museums. A tour of the **Vatican Gardens★** can be booked four days in advance at the Vatican Tourist Office ☎ 6988 4466 or 4866.

The Sistine Chapel, Raphael Rooms, Borgia Apartments, Apostolic Library, eight museums and five galleries are difficult to

View from the Vatican Palace over the gardens towards the Papal Academy.

see in one day. There are four colour-coded routes to help you round the exceptionally well organized art collections. One is a direct route to the always crowded Sistine Chapel. Here are highlights of other treasures:

Museo Egizio (Egyptian Museum)
Exhibits include burial chamber treasures from the Valley of the Kings, painted mummy-coffins, a baboon-god statue, and a marble sculpture of Emperor Hadrian's lover Antinous, drowned in the Nile.

Museo Pio-Clementino★★★
(Pio-Clementine Museum)
The 16 rooms contain classical antiquities,

Michelangelo's Pietà, in St Peter's Basilica, was completed when he was only 25.

notably **Laocoon★★★** (1C BC), a sculpture of the Trojan priest and his sons in a death-struggle with serpents in the Octagonal Belvedere Courtyard, and an Athenian **Belvedere Torso★★★** by Apollonius (50 BC) in the Hall of Muses, which inspired Michelangelo's nude forms for the Sistine Chapel frescoes.

Raphael's Expulsion of Heliodorus from the Temple shows Pope Julius II watching the thief Heliodorus being chased away (Raphael Rooms, Vatican).

Museo Gregoriano-Etrusco★
(Etruscan Museum)

This has elegant tomb sculptures dating from the 5C and 4C BC.

Stanze di Rafaello★★★ (Raphael Rooms)

These rooms are adorned with masterly

allegorical frescoes (1509–17). In the **School of Athens**, Raphael pays homage to Greek and Renaissance masters: at the centre Leonardo da Vinci as Plato, pointing to heaven, Michelangelo as Heraclitus, leaning on one elbow in the foreground, Bramante in the right corner as Euclid.

Cappella di Niccolò V★★
(Chapel of Nicholas V)
(signposted Cappella del Beato Angelico)
One of the oldest parts of the Vatican, this is decorated by Fra Angelico's gentle, stately frescoes (1447-51).

Pinacoteca★★★ (Picture Gallery)
Superb papal collections fill the 15 rooms, representing ten centuries of painting from the Byzantine era to the 18C, notably works by Giotto, Fra Angelico, Raphael, Bellini, Titian and Caravaggio.

Cappella Sistina★★★ (Sistine Chapel)
The chapel, traditionally used for the cardinals' conclave to elect a new pope, was built in 1484 for Pope Sixtus IV. The impact of **Michelangelo's frescoes** on the ceiling and altar-wall, brilliantly restored – for some, too brilliantly – is enough to overcome the discomfort of the crowds. Enjoy these masterpieces from the bench near the exit; sit back and take in the ceiling, if possible with binoculars, before looking more closely at the rest. The wall frescoes, including works by Botticelli, Ghirlandaio, Signorelli and Pinturicchio, narrate the Old and New Testament sagas of the world's destiny. Michelangelo's ceiling (1508–12) takes the story from Adam's creation to the Flood and Noah's drunkenness. Painted 23 years later,

Detail of The Expulsion of Adam and Eve from the Garden, by Michelangelo (from the ceiling of the Sistine Chapel).

the *Last Judgment* reveals his intense religious
faith, depicting Jesus as a fierce leader of
men. Below Jesus, the flayed skin of St
Bartholomew is Michelangelo's self-portrait.

Basilica di San Pietro*** (St Peter's Basilica)

Catholicism's principal church is built over the tomb of the apostle crucified in AD 64. A first basilica was erected here in 324, expanding over the next 12 centuries to become the biggest church in Christendom. By 1450, it threatened to collapse, but successive popes were reluctant to replace any part of the hallowed shrine. The advent of the tough Julius II in 1503 decided the matter: he built a new basilica.

The architects

The resulting grand edifice combines the concepts of a dozen architects over the next century. Donato Bramante took thousands of tons of marble and granite from the Colosseum and other ancient monuments for his centrally-planned Greek-cross design, beneath a unifying dome. At his death, Raphael took over and designed a long-naved basilica. Antonio da Sangallo the Younger brought back the Greek-cross plan, which Michelangelo in turn simplified for his dome. By 1606, the last major architect, Carlo Maderno, integrated Latin-cross and basilica plans with a long nave to meet Counter-Reformation demands for a vast congregation facing the pope enthroned at the west end.

A monumental landmark

The porticoed **façade** with long balcony makes the basilica look more like a palace than a church. From the piazza, the great **dome** is partly screened by the façade and best seen from an elevated viewpoint such as the Castel Sant'Angelo or Janiculum Hill. An outside elevator and stairs on the north side of the church take you to the top of the dome for a matchless panorama of Rome and Vatican City.

Statues

The basilica's most hallowed treasure, Michelangelo's **Pietà***** – the dead Christ on Mary's lap (1500) – is in a chapel to the right of the entrance (*see* p.58).
The faithful seek out on

the nave's right side the 13C bronze **statue of Peter**. Bronze was stripped from the Pantheon for the magnificent winding columns, said to be patterned after columns in the Temple of Solomon.

Bernini's bronze **St Peter's throne★★★**, has statues of the Church's founding fathers protecting remains of a seat perhaps used by the apostle.

The interior of St Peter's Basilica.

HISTORIC CENTRE
(CENTRO STORICO)

The historic heart of the city hugs a bend in the Tiber river where a Renaissance palace, a Baroque church and piazza and even some of the medieval Jewish Ghetto escaped the drastic urbanism rampant elsewhere in the city since 1870. Corso Vittorio Emanuele II (prolonging Via del Plebiscito from the Piazza Venezia) divides the historic centre into roughly even northern and southern halves, served by the famous Vatican-bound 64 bus from Stazione Termini.

THE SOUTHERN HALF

Piazza Venezia★★

Before escaping the turmoil of this unavoidable traffic junction, remember that the monstrous, bombastic **Vittorio Emanuele II Monument** (Il Vittoriano) is not a Fascist creation but an expression of 19C nationalism. Begun in 1885 and inaugurated in 1911, the Altar of the Nation, called 'the typewriter', commemorates united Italy's first king, Vittorio Emanuele II (on horseback at the centre). Its blindingly white Brescia marble jars against the Roman taste for warmer shades of ochre, amber or pink travertine.

The 15C Renaissance **Palazzo Venezia**★ on the west side of the square was the residence of Mussolini, who delivered his famous harangues from the balcony.

Piazza del Campidoglio★★★
(Capitol Square)

Michelangelo's elegant, harmonious design to crown Capitoline Hill was commissioned by Pope Paul III in 1536. From Piazza d'Aracoeli to the left (west) of the Vittoriano,

Looking across the Piazza Venezia to the Vittorio Emanuele II Monument.

the gently sloping Cordonata stairway enters the Renaissance square between giant statues of the twin demigods Castor and Pollux. Immediately across the almost imperceptibly cambered square is the 16C **Senatorial Palace★★★** (Palazzo Senatorio) reconstruction of a medieval fortress, now housing the city hall. **Conservators' Palace★★★** (Palazzo dei

Michelangelo designed both the broad staircase of the Cordonata and Capitol Square, creating an impressive approach to the Senatorial Palace beyond.

Conservatori) to the right and **New Palace** (Palazzo Nuovo) to the left together house the Capitoline Museums (*see* below). The great gilded bronze **equestrian statue of Marcus Aurelius** (2C AD) once in the centre of the piazza is now in the Palazzo Nuovo courtyard, protected by glass. Also there is the reclining figure of **Marforio**, one of Rome's *statue parlanti*, 'speaking statues', on which people traditionally posted civic complaints (*see* Piazza Navona, p.73).

Museo Capitolino★★ e Museo del Palazzo dei Conservatori★★★ (Capitoline Museums and Conservators' Palace Museum)

Outstanding among the Palazzo Nuovo's collection of classical antiquities are the

Dying Gaul★★★ and **Capitoline Venus**, both fine Roman copies of Greek originals, and the **dove mosaic**★★ from Hadrian's villa at Tivoli. Impressive portrait busts of emperors and philosophers are displayed in the halls. In the Palazzo dei Conservatori courtyard is the gigantic marble **head of Constantine**, from a colossus originally standing at his basilica in the Roman Forum. Other fragments come from the Capitol's Temple of Jupiter, which preceded the palace here. The best-known statue is the emblematic Etruscan bronze **She-Wolf** (5C BC), with the twins Romulus and Remus added by the Renaissance sculptor Antonio Pollaiolo (*see* p.10). The charming **Spinario**★★★ (1C BC), a boy removing a thorn from his foot, is

The Capitoline Museum contains dismembered parts of the huge colossus of Constantine.

67

When there is so much to see, it is always worth planning your route round the treasures of the Capitoline museums.

probably a Greek original. In the **Picture Gallery★** (Pinacoteca Capitolina) are two important Caravaggios, *John the Baptist* and *Fortune Teller*, Venetian works by Titian, Lotto, Veronese and Tintoretto, and portraits by Velazquez and Van Dyck.

Gesù Church★★★
West of Piazza Venezia, the Jesuits' principal church (1573) set the architectural pattern for the Counter-Reformation's campaign to seduce the people back from the Protestants. Giacomo della Porta's façade is more austere than later Baroque edifices,

but the glowing interior of gilt, bronze, precious stones and marble exalts the Catholic Church and its militant order. Most opulent is the **Chapel of St Ignatius Loyola** in which the tomb of the Jesuits' founder is adorned by a profusion of lapis lazuli.

Sant'Andrea della Valle★
Lying on the south side of Corso Vittorio Emanuele II, this admirable Baroque church boasts the city's second largest **dome★★** (after St Peter's). Giovanni Lanfranco painted the cupola's astonishing *Virgin in Glory* fresco while his rival, Domenichino, painted Evangelists on the pendentives and scenes from St Andrew's life in the apse.

Palazzo della Cancelleria★★
(Chancery Palace)
In sober contrast is the elegant late 15C Renaissance residence of Cardinal Raffaello Riario. The teenage churchman, grand-nephew of Pope Sixtus IV, paid for much of its costs from one hard night's gambling. Be sure to see the graceful porticoed courtyard.

Palazzo Farnese★★ (Farnese Palace)
Built for Cardinal Alexander Farnese before he became Pope Paul III, the city's grandest Renaissance palace now houses the French Embassy (not open to the public). Antonio da Sangallo the Younger designed the magnificent 16C façade and vestibule, with Michelangelo adding the central balcony, ornamental moulding of the cornices and the inner courtyard's upper storeys.

The palace's allegorical **frescoes** by Annibale and Agostino Carracci are one of the great treasures of late 16C painting. The piazza's two giant fountains are Egyptian

The fruit market at Campo dei Fiori offers an excellent selection of fresh produce for a picnic lunch.

granite basins from the Baths of Caracalla, adorned with the Farnese family's lily-of-the-valley coat of arms.

Piazza Campo dei Fiori★

People like the idea that the city's most charming market square, with lively cafés and bars, was once a flower meadow, but it was also notorious for its public executions. Surrounded by handsome ochre and russet façades, the 19C **statue of Giordano Bruno** marks the spot where the Inquisition burned the philosopher alive in 1600 for daring to suggest that ours was not the only galaxy in a universe that was infinite.

Campo dei Fiori is still the starting point for demonstrations in favour of uncomfortable ideas. **Palazzo Pio** is built on the ruins of Pompey's Theatre, scene of a more summary execution – the stabbing of Julius Caesar.

The Ghetto

Jews have lived in Rome since their first merchants arrived in the mid-2C BC. Abandoning their Trastevere homes in the 13C, they crossed the river to settle at the south end of the historic centre near the Tiber Island (Isola Tiberina). After centuries of relatively tolerant treatment, Pope Paul IV ordered public burnings of the Talmud and other sacred books and in 1555 turned their neighbourhood into a walled ghetto.

The wall on **Via del Portico d'Ottavia** has gone, but its medieval and Renaissance buildings remain a focus for the small modern Jewish community, and house its restaurants. The **Synagogue**, built in eclectic 'Neo-Babylonian' style in 1904, faces the river, with a small **museum** to tell the 2 000-year story.

Teatro di Marcello★★
(Theatre of Marcellus)

Begun by Julius Caesar and completed under Augustus in 11 BC, this theatre, with its fine tiers of Doric and Ionic arcades, inspired the design of the Colosseum and many Renaissance palaces. In the 16C, the home of circus games and gladiatorial combats was transformed into a palatial residence for the Roman aristocracy and their modern successors.

The church of Santa Maria in Cosmedin, with a fountain in the foreground.

Piazza Bocca della Verità★

The square is an enchanting blend of the city's historic character – two ancient temples (2C BC), a Romanesque church and Baroque fountain in a garden of umbrella pines. In the portico of **Santa Maria in**

*The famous Mouth
of Truth, in the
portico of the
church of Santa
Maria in Cosmedin.*

Cosmedin★★ church, visitors test the **Mouth
of Truth** (Bocca della Verità). Liars lose
their hands in what is actually an ancient
carved stone drain-cover (the Cloaca
Maxima sewer ends nearby). But admire,
too, the church's Romanesque campanile
and the interior's mosaic paving.

THE NORTHERN HALF

Piazza Navona★★★
More than any coin in the Trevi Fountain,
this handsomest of city squares is reason
enough for most people to return to Rome.
Tourists and Romans amble across the
round-ended oblong of what was once
Emperor Domitian's Circus Agonalis sports
stadium (AD 86). They sit around the
fountains, cafés and ice-cream parlours,

entertained by street musicians, clowns and fortune-tellers, charmed (or not) by artists of varying talent. At the centre, around an ancient obelisk, is Bernini's **Fountain of the Four Rivers★★★** (1651), a sculptural celebration of the Danube, the Ganges, the Rio de la Plata and the Nile – veiled for the mystery of its true source (*see* photo p.23).

The Piazza Navona, with the Fountain of the Moor (foreground) and the Baroque Sant'Agnese in Agone fronted by the Fountain of the Four Rivers.

The Baroque master's arch-rival, Francesco Borromini, designed the equally splendid church of **Sant'Agnese in Agone★★**. Beneath a gracefully elevated dome flanked by two campaniles, his concave façade gives the piazza its essential serenity. **Neptune's Fountain** to the north and the **Fountain of the Moor** to the south are 16C designs.

Until the 19C, the fountain outlets were blocked to flood the entire piazza for aquatic pageants in the summer, just as Renaissance tournaments had continued the site's sporting tradition.

Just south-west of Piazza Navona, on the little **Piazza di Pasquino**, is the most 'talkative' of Rome's speaking statues (*statue parlanti*), an ancient marble torso on which were posted the tailor Pasquino's scandalous comments on his Renaissance masters. These sparked off a satirical dialogue with

There is street art aimed at the tourist market for sale in the Piazza Navona.

The Fountain of Neptune, at one end of Piazza Navona, has the sea god as its centrepiece.

other statues like the Marforio on Campidoglio or the Facchino fountain off Via del Corso.

Caravaggio Masterpieces★★★
Two churches near Piazza Navona boast works of the greatest of 17C Lombard painters. In the Renaissance **St Augustine's Church★** (Sant'Agostino), admire the

intense compassion and surprising
sensuality of Caravaggio's *Madonna of the
Pilgrims*. In **San Luigi dei Francesi★★** his
three paintings of St Matthew reveal the raw
and simple truth of the untutored evangelist.

Sant'Ivo alla Sapienza★

The magnificent Baroque church, on Corso
del Rinascimento, was designed by
Borromini as a chapel for the university,
which was housed in Giacomo Della Porta's
Palazzo della Sapienza (now the State
Archives). Rising between two wings of the
palace's graceful porticoed courtyard, the
church's concave and convex surfaces,
characteristic Borromini features, blend
beautifully in façade and dome. The dome's
lofty lantern is thought to symbolize the
Tower of Babel.

The interior's intricate geometry forms a
star-like ground-plan with hexagon,
semicircle and triangle in beautiful harmony
with the great cupola, again emphasizing
the star motif as symbol of wisdom
(*sapienza*).

Piazza Sant'Ignazio★

Anyone doubting the theatrical inspiration
of Italian urban design will be convinced by
the sublime décor of this Rococo piazza.
Forming cosy alcoves or 'windows' on to
side-streets, all the 18C façades contribute to
the scenic harmony of the whole. More
austere is the façade of **Sant'Ignazio★★**
church, modelled – on a wider scale – after
its Jesuit mother church, Il Gesù (*see* p.21).
Inside, Andrea Pozzo, designer of the
founding Jesuit's tomb in Il Gesù, painted
the ceiling's splendid *trompe-l'oeil* fresco of
Ignatius' entry to heaven.

Pantheon★★★

Scholars consider Emperor Hadrian's domed temple, in the **Piazza della Rotonda**, a true masterpiece of Roman architecture. It was built in AD 118–125 after fires had ravaged an earlier structure of Augustus's son-in-law Agrippa, whose name is still inscribed above the Corinthian portico. A poultry market operated here in the Middle Ages, its stalls propped up in slots cut into the Egyptian granite columns. The artist Raphael was buried here at his request.

The fountain steps in Piazza della Rotonda are a favourite resting spot.

Scarcely visible from the outside, the temple's **dome★★★** imposes its full majesty from within. The hemispheric dome stands on a cylindrical drum of the same diameter, 43.3m (142ft). Evoking the vault of the heavens, the coffered cupola is pierced at the apex by an opening that provides the temple's only illumination. The aperture lets in a shaft of sunlight at varying angles throughout the day or, more spectacularly, a column of rain during a downpour.

Originally dedicated to Rome's 12 main deities, it became a church, St Mary of the Martyrs, in 609. Princes and popes stripped it of its marble and bronze, notably Urbain VII for Bernini's baldacchino in St Peter's and 80 cannons for Castel Sant'Angelo.

The majestic façade of the Roman temple, the Pantheon, is remarkably well-preserved.

FIVE MUSEUMS

Museo Borghese★★★
Villa Borghese
This recently restored museum houses works by such celebrated artists as Titian and Veronese. Also worth admiring are the impressive sculptures by **Bernini★★★** – the *Rape of Prosperpine, Appollo and Daphne,* and *David* sculpted when the artist was only 21. Some powerful paintings by the artist Caravaggio are exhibited on the first floor, including the sorrowful *David with Goliath's Head,* and the remarkable *Virgin and Child and St Anne* (**Madonna dei Palafrenieri★★★**).

Raphael's The Entombment (1507) can be seen in Museo Borghese.

Museo Nazionale della Villa Giulia★★★
(Villa Giulia National Museum)
Piazzale di Villa Giulia 9
This collection includes Etruscan terracotta
and stone tomb sculpture, pottery and
jewellery dating back to the 6C BC, housed
in Pope Julius III's handsome 16C summer
villa in the Borghese gardens.

Galleria Nazionale d'Arte Moderna★
(National Gallery of Modern Art)
Viale delle Belle Arti 131
Containing 20C art, this gallery in the
Borghese gardens includes the work of
Italian Futurists (Balla, Boccioni, Severini),
Modigliani, De Chirico and Morandi, as well
as Klee, Kandinsky, Max Ernst and Jackson
Pollock. Sculptors include Marino Marini,
Jean Arp, Giacometti and Henry Moore.

Palazzo Barberini★★ (Barberini Palace) and
Galleria Nazionale d'Arte Antica
(National Gallery of Antique Art)
Via delle Quattro Fontane 13
European painting from the 13C are housed
in this grand Baroque palace: Raphael's *La
Fornarina* (*see* p.25),Quentin Metsys'
Erasmus, Holbein's *Henry VIII* and works by
Titian, Caravaggio, El Greco and Tintoretto.

Galleria Doria Pamphili★★
Piazza del Collegio Romano 1A
This privately-owned collection of 400 works
includes works by the Carracci brothers,
Lorenzo Lotto, Titian, Guercino and
Caravaggio's uncommonly tranquil *Flight
into Egypt*. You can also see Velazquez's *Pope
Innocent X*, Pieter Bruegel's *Battle of Naples*,
and paintings by Rubens and Hans
Memling.

The basilica of Santa Maria Maggiore successfully combines a mixture of architectural styles.

FIVE CHURCHES

This section contains a selection of five historic churches outside the old centre.

Santa Maria Maggiore★★★ (St Mary Major)
The best conserved of Rome's early Christian churches (built 440); the simple form of the basilica is still discernible beneath the heavy Baroque ornament. Ferdinando Fuga designed the façade's elaborate portico and loggia in 1741 and the high altar's ornate canopy, inspired by Bernini's baldacchino for St Peter's. The church's outstanding **treasures★★★** are the

5C **mosaics** on the nave's upper walls and over the triumphal arch.

San Clemente★★
Different historical and architectural layers are visible in this church, which was built over a Roman palace and a 4C church. The beautiful 12C **mosaic★★★** in the apse shows the *Triumph of the Cross*, with delightful details. The restored Masolino **fresco★** in St Catherine's Chapel (Cappella di Santa Caterina) depicts the life of St Catherine of Alexandria. There are also 11C frescoes and 5C catacombs which are worth seeing.

San Giovanni in Laterano★★★
(St John Lateran)
The city's cathedral, seat of the pope as Bishop of Rome, was founded in 314, a year before St Peter's. It was repeatedly destroyed and rebuilt; the present formidable 18C façade is by Alessandro Galilei. The **bronze doors** are ancient originals from the Roman Curia. Inside, Borromini's restrained Baroque décor respects the spirit of the ancient basilica. Over the papal altar, a 14C **Gothic canopy** has silver reliquaries for the severed heads of Peter and Paul. Off the north aisle near the transept, visit the 13C **cloisters**, with charming mosaics and spiralling columns.

San Pietro in Vincoli★ (St Peter in Chains)
The chains of St Peter are the church's cherished relic, but its most prized treasure is Michelangelo's **Moses★★★** (1515). The awesome statue is part of Julius II's unfinished monumental tomb. The more placid statues of *Rachel* and *Leah* on either side were Michelangelo's last completed sculptures.

San Paolo Fuori le Mura★★
(St Paul Without the Walls)
Erected in the 4C over the apostle Paul's tomb outside the city walls, the church is second in size only to St Peter's, but poorly restored. Its majestic **interior★★★**, faithful to the basilica's original design, filters unique lighting through the translucent alabaster of the windows. Look for Arnolfo di Cambio's **Gothic ciborium★★★** over Paul's tomb, **Venetian mosaics** in the apse, and a delightful **cloister** (all 13C).

The 13C cloisters of St Paul Without the Walls have unusual twisted twin columns, and lovely mosaics.

WALKS
Here is a chance to stroll, not in quest of the Great Monument – though in Rome, they are not easily avoided – but to explore for yourself and make your own discoveries.

Monte Gianicolo★ (Janiculum Hill)
This park rewards you with the best **views★★★** over Rome and the Vatican. On the way, visit

the **Tempietto di Bramante★** (1511), an exquisite miniature masterpiece in the cloister of **San Pietro in Montorio★**. The temple's 16 Doric columns, balustrade and dome epitomize the Renaissance ideal of proportion and harmony. A more assertive monument is the **Acqua Paola fountain**, a 17C triumphal arch commanding a magnificent panorama over the city. Janiculum Hill was a bloody battlefield during the struggle for Italian unity in 1849 and busts of its 1000 heroes line the road to the **Garibaldi equestrian statue** at the top.

Pincio Gardens

From the top of the Spanish Steps (*see* p.31), make your way north along Viale Trinità dei Monti past the **Villa Medici**, home of the French Academy (where winners of the Prix de Rome studied). Its rather forbidding appearance conceals an ornate 17C façade overlooking gardens at the rear (visit Wednesday mornings). The Pincio gardens were laid out in 1818 by Giuseppe Valadier, including his own charming 'folly', **Casina Valadier**, with four different façades. The terrace of **Piazzale Napoleone** commands a magnificent view over Piazza del Popolo to the dome of St Peter's.

Trastevere★★

Historically working-class, the colourful neighbourhood 'across the Tiber' (*trans Tevere*) has old houses transformed into smart apartments, boutiques, galleries, restaurants and bars. A few old-timers keep alive the assertive spirit and give their name, *noantri* ('we others'), to the quarter's traditional summer festival.

From Piazza Sonnino, with its 13C feudal

85

Santa Maria in Trastevere has some beautiful mosaics, notably those by Cavallini depicting scenes from the life of the Virgin.

dungeon and Romanesque-Baroque church of San Crisogono, take Via della Lungaretta over to the main focus of neighbourhood life, **Piazza di Santa Maria in Trastevere★** and its Baroque fountain. The **church★★** has admirable 13C **mosaics★★★** on the façade and inside on the vault of the choir. To the north, bars and pizzerias abound on the bustling **Via della Scala**, surrounded by a maze of side-street workshops.

On the more aristocratic **Via della Lungara** is the grand 18C **Palazzo Corsini**, housing part of the National Gallery of Painting (Galleria Nazionale di Pittura): works by Caravaggio, Titian, Rubens and Canaletto. Opposite, set back from the road in beautiful gardens, is the 16C **Villa Farnesina**★★. This elegant Renaissance palace belonged to the Chigi bankers before passing to the Farnese cardinals. It is renowned for its **Raphael frescoes**.

Villa Borghese★★

Rome's most beautiful public gardens were created in the 17C by Cardinal Scipione Borghese, whose villa is now one of a group of museums (*see* p.80) set in the park's 86 hectares (212 acres). Romans come here for parties and picnics, boating and donkey rides, jogging and cycling (bicycle-hire, Villa Borghese car park). Finest of the park's summer houses is Pope Julius III's 16C **Villa Giulia** (*see* p.81). In the middle of the park amid cypresses and umbrella pines, the **Piazza di Siena** hippodrome offers an enchanting setting for equestrian shows.

The lovely gardens of the Villa Borghese offer a peaceful retreat from the bustle of the city.

EXCURSIONS FROM ROME

With so much to see inside the city, we have restricted excursions to four comfortable day-trips. COTRAL buses serve **Tivoli** and **Palestrina** east from Rebibbia metro station, **Castelli Romani** south-east from Anagnina and **Lake Bracciano** north from Lepanto.

Tivoli★★★

This vacation retreat – popular with both ancient and modern Romans – is the site of two palatial villas just 30km (19 miles) east of the capital along the Via Tiburtina.
Hadrian's Villa★★★ (Villa Adriana) One of Rome's ablest emperors, Hadrian built his home in AD 128, on what are now the town's southern outskirts at the foot of the Sabine Hills. Its romantic gardens sprawl across 70 hectares (173 acres), with wild cypresses, pines and olive trees growing among the arches, columns and mosaic paving of the pavilions, Greek and Latin libraries, temples, Greek theatre and monumental baths. The **Teatro Marittimo★★★** is the centrepiece, with its circular portico and dreamy reflecting pool.
Villa d'Este★★★ The opulent 16C residence of Cardinal Ippolito d'Este, son of Lucrezia Borgia, has some fine Correggio frescoes. But it is better known for its gardens, an extravagant spectacle with some 500 fountains, including Bernini's **Fontana dell'Ovato★★★** and **Fontana dell'Organo★★★**, grottoes, waterfalls and ponds.

Palestrina

This pretty town of Etruscan origin has recovered well from World War II bombing. Indeed, the destruction laid bare remains of the ancient **Tempio della Fortuna Primigenia★**, over which the medieval town

was built. The 17C **Palazzo Barberini**, built directly over the main temple, houses a **museum** (museo archeologico prenestino) with bronze and terracotta tomb sculpture, jewellery and ceramics from the nearby

The Fontana dell'Organo in the gardens of Villa d'Este.

necropolis. The **Nile Mosaic★★** (2C BC) from the temple's inner sanctum depicts the river's wildlife, along with ancient rituals and banquets. A modern statue in front of the cathedral celebrates Giovanni Pierluigi da Palestrina, the 16C composer of polyphonic church music who was born here.

Castelli Romani

The 'Roman fortresses' which give the region its name were medieval strongholds built on the Alban Hills (Colli Albani) south-east of Rome. Now it is the vineyards and lakes that draw the day-trippers.

Frascati★

Surrounded by hillside Renaissance villas, the best known of the wine towns offer light whites that taste better here, in the cool of a cellar, with a slice of ham or sausage, than back in a Roman tourist-trap. Visit the gardens of the **Villa Aldobrandini★** (1603).

Lake Albano★

On the wooded slopes above Lake Albano is the pope's summer retreat at **Castel Gandolfo★** – he gives papal audiences on Wednesdays and blessings for pilgrims at Sunday noon. The town of **Ariccia** is famous for its roast suckling pig, *porchetta*.

Lake Bracciano★★

This large freshwater lake, formed from volcanic craters, has several pretty villages and good facilities for water sports. Some 40km (25 miles) north of Rome, **Bracciano★** is the main town, with an imposing 15C **castle★★★**. For fine views, climb up to **Anguillara-Sabazia★** on its craggy promontory overlooking the lake.

GAZETTEER

Ara Pacis Augustae★★ (Via di Ripetta) This modern reconstruction of Augustus' Altar of Peace (9 BC) has fragments of the original frieze.

Aventino★ A quiet residential area south of Circus Maximus, with pretty gardens, parks of palms and pines, and early Christian churches (**Santa Sabina**★★).

Baths of Diocletian (Piazza della Repubblica) This building (AD 306) now incorporates the church of St Mary of the

The ancient Appian Way still has the original Roman paving, and is lined with the ruins of the tombs of those buried along the route in Roman times.

Angels (**Santa Maria degli Angeli★★**) and the National Roman Museum (**Museo Nazionale Romano delle Terme★★★** – currently being restored).

Borgia Apartments★ (Vatican) This six-roomed suite contains frescoes by Pinturicchio painted for Pope Alexander VI (Rodrigo Borgia, father of Cesare and Lucrezia).

Catacombs★★ These contain ancient Roman, Jewish and Christian burial vaults: San Callisto (early popes), San Sebastiano (frescoes)and Domitilla (1C and 2C AD; frescoes).

Cinecittà Recently, these studios have become TV- rather than movie-oriented (originally built by Mussolini); guided tours can be arranged by appointment ☎ 722 931.

Circus Maximus (Circo Massimo) This grass-covered chariot-race track built by Julius Caesar for 300 000 spectators, is now the vast centre of a traffic circle.

Cloaca Maxima An Etruscan-built sewer; the outlet is visible from Ponte Palatino.

EUR – Esposizione Universale di Roma Sprawling fairgrounds, planned under Mussolini and completed in the 1960s, include the Palazzo dei Congresso, Palazzo dello Sport and **il museo della Civiltà Romana★★**.

Fontana delle Naiadi – (Piazza della Repubblica) Sexy nymphs adorn this Art Nouveau fountain (1885).

Fori Imperiali★★★ Disparate ruins north of the Roman Forum, built by Julius Caesar and early emperors. They include **Trajan's Column★★★** (Colonna Traiana) – a beautifully restored 38m (124ft) monument celebrating victories over the Dacians, and **Trajan's Markets**, a well-preserved

Trajan's Column; the statue of Trajan on the top was replaced with one of St Peter in 1587.

semicircular shopping mall (*see* p.98).
Foro Italico (Lungotevere Maresciallio Diaz) Mussolini's sports complex, used for the Olympics and the Italian Tennis Open.
Fosse Ardeatine (Via Appia Antica) Quarry monument to 335 Italians shot there by the Nazis in 1944.
Mausoleum of Augustus (Via di Ripetta) The Emperor Augustus's cylindrical family tomb was restored by Mussolini, perhaps for himself.

Mura Aureliane (Aurelian Wall) Built around the city centre by Emperor Aurelian (AD 270, the best preserved section of the wall is between the Pincio and Borghese gardens.

Museo Barracco (Corso Vittorio Emanuele 168) This museum has a fine collection of Greek, Babylonian, Egyptian and Roman sculpture.

Museo del Folklore (Piazza Sant'Egidio, Trastevere) Contains costumes and waxwork models of 18C and 19C Roman street life, taverns and shops.

Palatino★★★ The ruins south of the Roman Forum incorporate the Farnese Gardens (Orti Farnesiani) among the emperors' palaces of **Domus Flavia★**, **Domus Augustana★★** and the House of Livia (Augustus's wife).

Palazzo Madama (Corso del Rinascimento) This 16C and 17C Medici palace now houses the Italian Senate.

Palazzo Quirinale★★ (Quirinal Palace) This huge former 16C papal summer palace (east of the Trevi fountain) is now the presidential residence.

Palazzo Spada★ (Piazza Capo di Ferro) South of Campo dei Fiori, this 16C palazzo has Borromini's *trompe l'oeil* colonnaded gallery and 17C paintings.

Piazza Barberini Bernini's **Fontana del Tritone★**, showing the Triton with a conch shell, is in the centre of the square. Tucked away in a corner is his Fontana delle Api, the fountain of bees (Pope Urban VIII's emblem).

Piazza della Minerva (Near the Pantheon) Look for Bernini's marble elephant supporting an Egyptian obelisk (Pulcino della Minerva)

Piramide di Caio Cestio★ (Pyramid of Caius Cestius) (Piazza di Porta San Paolo) This

modest but impressive white marble tomb of the Roman magistrate, Caius Cestius, was built in 12 BC.

Portico di Ottavia (North edge of the Ghetto) Built by Augustus for his sister, Octavia, the only surviving portico of the piazza of Circus Flaminius is now incorporated into the façade of Sant'Angelo in Pescheria church.

Protestant Cemetery (Via Caio Cestio 6) Wander round the monuments and look for non-Catholics, including the poets Keats and Shelley, and Communist Antonio Gramsci, who rest here.

San Carlo alle Quattro Fontane★★ (Via del Quirinale) This oval-domed Baroque church (also known as San Carlino) was Borromini's first commission (1634), and has a superb interior.

Left: Bernini's famous elephant supports the Egyptian obelisk in Piazza della Minerva.

Right: The Pyramid of Caius Cestius is 27m (89ft) high and took 330 days to build.

95

San Lorenzo fuori le Mura★★ (Piazzale del Verano) An early Christian basilica, with portico with sarcophagi, mosaics and a 12C throne.

Sant'Andrea al Quirinale★★ (Via del Quirinale 29) A fine example of Bernini's Roman Baroque, with a roseate marble **interior**★★.

Santa Cecilia in Trastevere★ Built on the 5C AD martyr's house, the church has lovely mosaics. Stefano Maderno's exquisite sculpture (high altar) of Cecilia's body was said to have been carved using as a model her undecayed body which was disinterred in 1599.

Santa Maria della Pace★ (Via della Pace) Look for Bramante's Renaissance cloister, the Baroque façade, and inside, Raphael's *Sibyl* frescoes.

Santa Maria della Vittoria★★ (Via XX Settembre) See Bernini's Cornaro Chapel sculpture of **St Teresa's Ecstasy**★★★.

Santa Maria d'Aracoeli★★ (Campidoglio) Contains the 13C mosaic paving over the Temple of Juno, home of the sacred geese that warned of the attack by Gaul in 390 BC.

Santa Maria sopra Minerva★★ (Piazza della Minerva) Rome's lone Gothic church.

Santa Prassede★ Behind the unprepossessing exterior are some fine Byzantine mosaics, brilliant 9C works by artists from Constantinople. The best are of Jesus and four angels in the Chapel of **St Zeno**★★ and the *New Jerusalem* over the triumphal arch.

Santa Sabina (Piazza Pietro d'Illiria) Note the 5C original carved cypress wood doors, mosaics, and the 13C cloister.

Santi Cosma e Damiano (St Cosmas and St Damian) (Via dei Fori Imperiali) Built against the Roman Forum's Temple of

The Aracoeli Staircase, built in 1346 to give thanks for Rome being spared the plague, leads up to the church of Santa Maria in Aracoeli.

Romulus, this church has 6C and 7C mosaics and a Neapolitan crib.

Santi Giovanni e Paolo (Colosseum area) This Romanesque church has ancient frescoes which are now being restored.

Teatro Argentina (Largo di Torre Argentina 52) This is the beautiful, newly restored home of the Teatro di Roma.

Testaccio This colourful working-class neighbourhood, south of the Aventine, also has a lively food market on Piazza Testaccio.

Tiber Island★ (Isola Tiberina) Linked to the river banks by the Fabricio and Cestio bridges, this is the site of the Fatebenefratelli hospital founded in the 16C.

Vatican Library (access by written application to the *Prefettura*) This fine collection contains over a million books, manuscripts and medieval treasures.

Via Appia Antica★★ (Appian Way) This south-bound road, begun 312 BC, goes past the

In the 2C AD, Emperor Trajan built a complex of 150 shops and offices, selling everything from fine Oriental silks to fruit and fish – the Roman equivalent of our modern-day shopping complex.

Porta San Sebastiano, passing the Catacombs, Circus of Maxentius and Tomb of Cecilia Metella (*see* p.91).

Via del Governo Vecchio (parallel to Corso Vittorio Emanuele II) This is a good area to wander and browse the colourful workshops, and is good for second-hand clothes, lace, and a choice of cheaper restaurants.

Via Veneto★ (Via Vittorio Veneto) Another street to enjoy at a leisurely pace, starting from Piazza Barberini. You will find smart bars, hotels, and the US Embassy is still there, but the spirit of *La Dolce Vita* has gone.

Villa Doria Pamphili This huge 17C park, south of the Vatican, offers formal gardens and wild pine woods.

ENJOYING YOUR VISIT

Weather

Rome is at its mellow best – warm days and cool evenings – in April and May and again from September to mid-October. There are two provisos: Easter packs the town with pilgrims, overloading hotels and restaurants, and October can be very wet.

The hot weather begins in June, and even Romans find July and August unbearably hot – in the high 90°s Fahrenheit (36°C) at noon – and get out of the city whenever possible, leaving a ghost-town by *Ferragosto* (15 August). Winters are rainy and cool rather than cold, though freezing point is not uncommon in January.

Calendar of Events

In addition to the national public holidays (marked by an asterisk), the city has a host of feasts, festivals, art and fashion shows:

1 January*: New Year's Day (*Capodanno*)

6 January*: Epiphany (*La Befana*); climax of the Children's Fair on Piazza Navona

February/March: *Carnevale*, Mardi Gras parties for adults, costumes and confetti for the children, processions in Castelli Romani

March/April – Easter Holy Week (*Settimana Santa*): Palm Sunday Mass in St Peter's Square; Maundy Thursday papal mass at San Giovanni in Laterano; Good Friday papal mass at the Colosseum, Stations of the Cross procession on the Palatine; Easter Sunday *Urbi et Orbi* blessing in St Peter's Square; *Easter Monday (*Pasquetta*) country picnics

21 April: Campidoglio pageant and Aventine fireworks for Rome's 'foundation' in 753 BC

25 April*: Liberation Day – wreath-laying at the Vittoriano; remembrance of the Nazi

massacre at Fosse Ardeatine mausoleum
April/May: Horse Show at Piazza di Siena, in the Villa Borghese gardens
1 May*: Labour Day (*Festa del Lavoro*), rock concert in Piazza San Giovanni; country picnics
May: Italian Tennis Open, Foro Italico; Spring Antiques Fair, Via dei Coronari; Spring Art Fair, Via Margutta
July-September: *Estate Romana* summer cultural festival – theatre, film, music and dance all over town
July: *Roma Alta Moda*, high fashion week, Piazza di Spagna; *Festa de Noantri* folk festival in Trastevere
15 August*: Assumption (*Ferragosto*); everybody leaves town
October: Autumn Antiques Fair, Via dei Coronari; Autumn Art Fair, Via Margutta
1 November*: All Saints' Day (*Ognissanti*)
8 December*: Feast of the Immaculate Conception, flowers on Piazza di Spagna's Madonna
24 December: Midnight Mass at St Peter's
25 December*: Quiet Christmas festivities
26 December*: *Santo Stefano*

Food and Drink

Compared to Bologna, say, or Genoa, Rome is not a temple of high gastronomy. Romans have inherited the tastes not of their aristocrats, a generally disreputable bunch, but of the common people. This *cucina povera* – cuisine of the poor – brings rich flavour to the simplest ingredients of pork, sausage, tripe, salt cod, artichokes, beans, but also a wide and healthy assortment of salads and green vegetables. No refined sauces or delicate blends of taste, but hearty portions for strong stomachs, all served in a

raucous, festive atmosphere, not with the hushed reverence reserved for high cuisine.

By the same token, when choosing a place to eat, remember that food in the simplest *trattoria* or family *osteria* is nearly always better and more authentic than in the self-important *ristorante*, with its pretentious décor and prices to match. Along with a cover charge (*pane e coperto*), service is included in the bill (*ricevuta fiscale*) which the establishment is legally obliged to give you. An extra tip is customary – up to 10% – but not expected in a family-run place. Ideal for a quick lunch, the Italian 'snack bar', *tavola calda*, serves toasted sandwiches and other hot or cold snacks at the counter.

Pasta is often a central ingredient for a typical Italian meal.

Terrace cafés are very popular in Rome, especially on warm summer evenings. Here are a few suggestions:

Caffè Greco, 86 via dei Condotti
Antico della Pace, via della Pace Caffè
Doney et Caffè de Paris, via Veneto
Bar Tre Scalini, piazza Navona
Caffè Rosati et Caffè Canova, piazza del Popolo
Caffè S. Eustachio, piazza S. Eustachio.

For a more 'complete' meal, the following courses are usually served.

Antipasti (hors d'oeuvres)

The only real Roman antipasto is *Suppli alla romana* – deep-fried rice-balls filled with ragu. You will also find *peperoni*, red, yellow and green peppers grilled and marinated in olive oil, *zucchine* and *finocchi* (sliced fennel), or ham and salami.

Primi piatti

Roman-style **pasta** is very often spaghetti at its simplest *all'aglio e olio*, in garlic and olive oil, spicy *all'amatriciana* with salt pork and tomatoes or *alla carbonara*, with eggs, salt pork and black pepper. *Tagliatelle* ribbon noodles are *fettucine* in Rome, often just mixed with butter, cheese and black pepper. *Gnocchi alla Romana* is gnocchi cooked in the oven. A popular local **soup** is *stracciatella*, a clear broth with grated cheese and an egg beaten into it.

Secondi piatti

These dishes usually consist of fish or meat and vegetables. They include the famous sliced veal wrapped around ham and sage, cooked in white wine and just big enough to 'jump into the mouth' – *saltimbocca*. And Romans' appetites are too robust to shed a sentimental tear when devouring roast suckling pig (*porchetta*), baby lamb

(*abbacchio*), roast kid (*capretto*) or oxtail
(*coda alla vaccinara*).

Vegetables (contorni)

Pride of place among the vegetables goes to
green artichokes: *carciofi alla giudia*, deep-
fried Jewish-style, or *carciofi alla Romana*,
stewed in oil and garlic.

Dessert (formaggio/frutta/dolce o dessert)

Apart from a few grapes (*uva*) or figs (*fichi*)
or cheese, this is not a Roman restaurant
speciality. People often have an extra-strong
espresso ristretto and take an after-dinner stroll
to the nearest ice-cream parlour (*gelateria*).

Wines

While there are no particular specialities
from Rome itself, Italy offers a good
selection of wines from its various regions.

*No trip to Rome is
complete without
sampling delicious
Italian ice-cream.*

Here are a few restaurants to try:
Da Pancrazio, piazza del Biscione 92,
☎ 6861246. Built on Pompee theatre ruins.
Apuleius, via del Tempio di Diana 15,
☎ 5742160.
Costanza, piazza del Paradiso 63/65,
☎ 6861717.
Osteria dell'Angelo, via Zettolo 24,
☎ 3729470. Roman cuisine.
Marchetti, via del Pantheon 36, ☎ 67844017.
Bar service, wine by the glass, cheeses.

*There are many
open-air cafés
where you can rest
and refresh
yourself, often in
imposing settings
such as this one in
the Pantheon area.*

Trattoria Perilli, via Marmorata 39,
☎ 5742415. Specialities of Rome.
Osteria Sagra del Vino, via Marziale 5,
☎ 39737015. Roman specialities.
Bottega del Vino di Anacleto Zleve, via Santa
Maria del Pianto 9/a, via Santa Maria
☎ 6865970. Cold dishes, wine by the glass if
preferred.

Shopping

Vanity is an Italian virtue. People shop to
look good, cut a fine figure – *una bella figura*.
Rome is the perfect place to indulge your
own narcissism.

High Fashion

If 'sense of style' is an essential part of the
national genius, the streets around **Spanish
Square** are a perfect showcase for it. Even if
you are not in the market for the silks, shoes,
jewellery or sleekest of leatherware, the
window displays themselves are sheer works

*Via Condotti has
some of Rome's top
designer shops, and
is a popular haunt
for evening strolls.*

of art. **Via Condotti** and **Via Borgognona** are the most hallowed sanctuaries of luxury and its high priests are Bulgari and Gucci.

Street Fashion

More popularly priced clothes – jeans, leather jackets, sweaters and boots – are to be found on **Via del Corso** and **Via Tritone**.

Art, Antiques and Flea Markets

Running north of Spanish Square, **Via del Babuino** and **Via Margutta** are famous for their antique shops and art galleries. More moderately priced antiques can be found on **Via dei Coronari,** near Piazza Navona.

If you are more interested in curios, bric-à-brac or stylish junk, go to Trastevere's **Porta Portese** on Sunday mornings. For second-hand clothing and camping equipment, try **Via Sannio**.

The colourful flea market at Porta Portese is full of interesting curios and mementos.

Food Markets

For your picnic in the park, **Campo dei Fiori** has a delightful fruit and vegetable market; mornings, Monday to Saturday. The one on **Piazza Vittorio Emanuele II** is bigger and noisier, but excellent for cheeses, salami, hams and exotic tropical foods.

Entertainment and Nightlife

For details of the constantly changing scene, check *Il Messaggero* and *La Repubblica*'s Thursday entertainment guide, *Trovaroma*. The EPT tourist office publishes lists of events in its monthly *Carnet di Roma*.

Classical Music

The prestigious **Accademia di Santa Cecilia** holds its summer season of symphonic and chamber music in the beautiful open-air setting of the 16C Villa Giulia in the Borghese Gardens. From October to June, it performs at the Auditorio Pio, Via della Conciliazione. The **Accademia Filarmonica Romana** divides its season (September to May) between its own Sala Casella concert hall, Via Flaminia 118, and the modern Teatro Olimpico, Piazza Gentile da Fabriano.

Opera and Ballet

The summer season at the **Baths of Caracalla** is one of Europe's great spectacles, despite complaints of a recent decline in the quality of performances by the **Teatro dell'Opera**. The repertoire is usually a popular one, typically Verdi's *Aida*, Puccini's *Tosca* and Bizet's *Carmen*. The winter season, December to May, is held at the opera hall, Via Firenze 72, with a longer season of recitals, from November to June. **Classical ballet** is held at the Teatro dell'Opera from December to June, while a **modern dance** season (September-May) is held at the Teatro Olimpico.

Rock and Jazz

Two major events are a day-and-night **May Day Rock Festival** (free) at Piazza San Giovanni, and a summer **Jazz Festival**, usually from the end of June, at the Foro Italico. Live bands perform in bars in the lively **Testaccio** neighbourhood.

Nightlife

Federico Fellini made *La Dolce Vita* nearly 40 years ago and the café society life it symbolized ground to a halt shortly afterwards. Since then, the remaining nightclubs on and around **Via Veneto** have become high-priced tourist traps. Roman sophisticates have moved over to bars around **Via della Pace** and **Piazza delle Copelle**, north of the Pantheon, or retreated to artists' hangouts in **Trastevere**.

The younger crowd prefers the action around **Piazza Navona** and **Campo dei Fiori**, although 'action' is perhaps too energetic a word for the preferred activity of standing around and looking at each other during the evening stroll (*passegiata*).

Discos come and go, some of the liveliest being in outlying neighbourhoods like working class Testaccio south of the Aventine, or bourgeois Parioli north of the Villa Borghese. Many set up in the summer as beach discos out at Fregene and Ostia.

Sports

Apart from **swimming** in pools at the major hotels and **watersports** out at Lake Bracciano (*see* p. 90), there is little opportunity for active sports in Rome unless you are a member of a private club. If **golf** is your sport, your hotel may help you gain access to the exclusive Circolo del Golf di Roma on the Via Appia Antica, at least for some

The ritual of the evening passeggiata is an important element of life in Rome, just as it is throughout Italy.

driving practice. If you feel the need for some exercise, try **jogging** along the Tiber or around the gardens of the Villa Borghese.

Rome has more to offer in the way of spectator sports. Rome's two professional **football** (**calcio**) teams play their home games on alternative weeks at the 100 000-capacity Stadio Olimpico, Via dei Gladiatori. Rivalry is fierce between the two teams – *Roma* and *Lazio* – and spectators become very animated. Yet even in the heated atmosphere, foreign spectators are treated with remarkable good humour.

Gaining in popularity, **basketball** (*il basket*) is played in the magnificent Palazzo dello Sport, designed by Pier Luigi Nervi for the 1960 Olympics.

THE BASICS

Before You Go

Visitors entering Italy should have a full passport, valid to cover the period in which they will be travelling. No visa is required for members of EU countries, the United States, Canada, Australia and New Zealand. No vaccinations are necessary.

Getting There

International flights arrive at Leonardo da Vinci Airport, near Fiumicino, 30km (19 miles) from Rome, and mainly charter flights land at Ciampino, which is 15km (9 miles) from the city.

Trains arrive at Rome's main railway station, Stazione Termini, from many continental destinations as well as other major Italian cities. The EuroCity service connects the main European cities to Rome by a very fast service, and there is a sleeper and couchette service between Paris and Rome, and from various continental ports and towns. Holders of an InterRail card receive large reductions on the cost of their rail travel.

Frequent coach services carry passengers from London and other European cities to Rome, arriving at the Piazza della Repubblica in the capital.

Driving to Rome can be an enjoyable exercise if have the time; routes from the east are now limited by the problems in former Yugoslavia, but there are many entry points from the north and north-west, such as Ventimiglia (from France), the St Bernard pass (from Switzerland) and the Brenner pass (from Austria).

Arriving

Trains link Leonardo da Vinci airport with the central station, Stazione Termini, about every 40 minutes, and the fare costs around 12 000 lire (about £4.80/$7.70). The easiest way to reach the city is by a taxi, a ride of about 30 minutes which can increase dramatically during the rush hour. Taxis cost in the region of 60 000 lire (£24/$38). From Ciampino there is a bus service to Anagnina Metro station, and metro connections can be made from there to Stazione Termini. A taxi from Ciampino into the city costs about 50 000 lire (£20/$32).

Within three days of arriving in Italy, all foreign nationals must register with the police. If you are staying in a hotel, the management will normally attend to this formality, but the visitor is responsible for checking that it has been carried out.

There is no limit on the importation into Italy of tax-paid goods bought in an EU country provided they are for personal consumption, with the exception of alcohol and tobacco which have fixed limits governing them.

An artist at work in one of Rome's many squares.

A-Z

Accidents and Breakdowns

In case of a breakdown ☎ 116 and the operator will send an ACI (Italian Automobile Club) service vehicle. A red warning triangle should be placed 50m (165ft) behind the vehicle, and your hazard warning lights switched on. In the event of an accident, exchange names, addresses and insurance details. To contact the police or ambulance, ☎ 113. There are emergency telephones at 1km (0.6 mile) intervals along the motorways (*autostrade*).

Fully comprehensive insurance is advisable for motorists in Italy, and motoring organizations recommend that you carry a green card, although this is no longer a legal requirement.

Accommodation

For information on hotels and restaurants in Rome, refer to the *Michelin Red Guides Italia* and *Europe*. Italian hotels are classified from one to five stars, and Rome is well supplied with accommodation in all classes, including guest houses (*pensioni*). The average double room with private bath/shower in a three-star hotel costs around 200 000-300 000 lire; breakfast is usually extra. Centrally located hotels are very much in demand, and it is advisable to book well in advance of your visit, particularly in the summer, or at Easter or Christmas.

The tourist information offices at Leonardo da Vinci Airport, Termini station, and Via Parigi 5 offer a free accommodation service, and have a list of hotels which can be ordered if you want to book in advance.

Apply to International Services in Via del Babuino 79 for details of self-catering studios and apartments; ☎ 360 00018/19. For travellers on a tight budget there is the option of staying cheaply in a religious house where rooms are normally reserved for pilgrims. Two such places

Looking across to St Peter's Basilica at sunset.

near the Vatican are: Domus Mariae, ☎ **662 3138**, and Instituto Madri Pie, ☎ **631 967**. Book early, especially if your visit coincides with a religious festival or holiday.

A new concept for Rome is Italian Bed & Breakfast. Rate: 50,000l to 90,000l for a single, 90,000l for a double (without bathroom) on the outskirts, to 150,000l (with bathroom) in the city centre. Internet address: www.b-b.rm.it, or to book ☎ **39 6 687 7348**

Some good value hotels:
Teatro di Pompeo, Largo del Pallaro 8, ☎ **68300170**.
Campo dei Fiori, via del Biscione 6, ☎ **68806865**. Romantic, with terrace overlooking Rome.
Alimandi, via Tunisi 8. Near the Vatican Museum, ☎ **723948**

Family hotel with terrace.
Igea, via Principe amadeo 97, ☎ **4466913**. In the Central Station area.
Mozart, via dei Greci 23/b. Family hotel, well placed for shopping
San Anselmo, piazza San Anselmo 2, ☎ **5748119**. In the Aventino Hill area with garden.
Villa San Pio, via San Anselmo 198, ☎ **5743547**. On Aventino Hill.
Santa Prisca, via M. Gelsomini 25, ☎ **5750469**. Hotel managed by nuns.
Amalia, via Germanico 76, ☎ **39723354**. San Pietro area.
Sole, via del Biscione 76, ☎ **68806873**. Near Piazza Navona. Quiet.
Celio, via dei Santissimi 4 35/c, ☎ **70495333**. Near the

Colosseum. Family hotel. Rooms decorated with frescoes. *Casa tra Noi*, via Monte del Gallo 113. ☎ 39387355. Quiet. Basic.

The only youth hostel run by the YHA in Rome is the Ostello del Foro Italico, Viale della Olimpiadi 61,☎ 324 2613 or 323 6279, which is reserved for YHA members. There are two hostels for women in the city: the YWCA is at Via Balbo 4, ☎ 488 3917 or 488 0460, and for young women under 25, the Protezione della Giovane at Via Urbana 158, ☎ 488 1489 or 488 0056, can find rooms.

There are no campsites within the city, but there are four on the approach roads into Rome (*see* **Camping**)

Banks

Banks are open from 8.30am-1.30pm, Monday to Friday, and for one hour in the afternoon, usually 3-4pm. They are closed at weekends. Tourists can change money at main railway stations and airports, and travellers' cheques and cheques can be changed at most hotels.

Bicycles

Roman roads are full of traffic, often travelling at great speeds. In such dangerous conditions, cycling is not recommended.

Breakdowns see Accidents

Camping

Camping is very popular in Italy, and there are over 2 000 sites across the country. None are in Rome itself, but there are four sites on the approach roads to the city, just a short bus ride away:
Nomentano Via della Cesarina 11; *Campidoglio* Ostia Antica, Via Castelfusano 195 ☎ 566 2720; *Roma* Via Aurelia 831 ☎ 622 3018; and *Flaminio* Via Flaminia, Nuova 821 ☎ 333 2604.

For details of other campsites write to the office of the Italian State Tourist Board in your home country. *See* **Tourist Information Offices**

Car Hire

Rome is well stocked with car-hire agencies, and there are outlets at airports, air terminals and railway stations as well as in the city centre. Airlines and tour operators offer fly/drive arrangements, and car hire in conjunction with train travel is also available through some of the major car hire companies.

Weekly rates with unlimited mileage offer the best deal; these include breakdown service and basic insurance, but you are advised to take out a collision damage waiver and personal accident insurance. Small local firms generally offer the cheapest rates, but they can only be booked locally. Most hire companies restrict hire of cars to drivers over 21.

Drivers must have held their full licence for at least a year. With the exception of Avis, there is an upper age limit of 60/65. Unless paying by credit card a substantial cash deposit is required. Full details of the different hire schemes can be obtained from tourist offices. *See also* **Accidents and Breakdowns**, and **Tourist Information Offices**

Children

Rome is not the ideal city to take young children to, being busy, hot and noisy, but there are parks with playgrounds such as the Villa Borghese, Villa Ada and Villa Glori. At EUR there is the largest amusement park in Italy, just 5km (3 miles) out of the city and reachable by bus from Stazione Termini.

Children under four not occupying a seat travel free on Italian railways; between the ages of four and 12, they get a reduction of 50 per cent.

Baby food can be bought at a chemist's (*farmacia*), or at supermarkets and grocers.

Babysitting can often be arranged by your hotel or pensione. Otherwise try the babysitting agencies at: ARCI Donna Roma, ☎ **31 6449**; Centri di Solidarietà, ☎ **428 0321**; or La Ciliegia, ☎ **627 5705**.

Climate *see* **p. 99**

Clothing

Spring and autumn are warm and pleasant times of the year to visit Rome, and during those months light clothes can be worn in the day, with a sweater or jacket for the evenings and cooler days. The summer can be sweltering, and feels even hotter than it is because of the large numbers of people and the narrow streets. If you must sightsee during July and August, wear as few clothes as possible, but remember to cover up shoulders (and upper body for men) and upper legs when visiting churches.

Italian clothing measurements differ from those in the UK, the US and some other European countries. The following are examples:

Dress Sizes

UK	8	10	12	14	16	18
Italy	38	40	42	44	46	18
US	6	8	10	12	14	16

Men's Suits

UK/US	36	38	40	42	44	46
Italy	46	48	50	52	54	56

Men's Shirts

UK/US	14	14.5	15	15.5	16	16.5	17
Italy	36	37	38	39/40	41	42	43

Men's Shoes

UK	7	7.5	8.5	9.5		10.5	11
Italy	41	42	43	44		45	46
US	8	8.5	9.5	10.5		11.5	12

Women's Shoes

UK		4.5	5	5.5	6		6.5	7
Italy		38	38	38	39		39	40
US		6	6.5	7	7.5		8	8.5

Complaints

Make any complaint at a hotel, shop or restaurant to the manager in a calm manner. For more serious complaints, contact the *Polizia* on ☎ **4686**, ext **2102** or **2876**, or report your problem to the tourist office (*see* **Tourist Information Offices**).

Consulates

Embassies and consulates can be found at the following addresses:

British Consulate:
Via XX Settembre 80a;
☎ **482 5441** or **482 5551**.

Irish Consulate:
Largo del Nazareno 3;
☎ **678 2541.**

Australian Embassy:
Via Alessandria 215;
☎ **854 2721**.

Canadian Embassy:
Via GB De Rossi 27;
☎ **445 981**.

New Zealand Embassy:
Via Zara 28;
☎ **440 2928**.

United States Embassy:
Via Veneto 119a;
☎ **46741**.

Crime

As in many of the world's towns and cities, Rome is a target for gangs of pickpockets. Without wanting to be alarmist, the best advice is to be aware at all times, carry as little money and as few credit cards as possible, and leave any valuables in the hotel safe.

Carry wallets and purses in secure pockets inside your outer clothing, wear body belts, or carry handbags across your body or firmly under your arm. Never leave your car unlocked, and hide away or remove items of value.

If you have anything stolen, report it immediately to the police. A special police information office where tourists may get assistance is available on ☎ **4686**, ext **2102** or **2876**. Collect a report so that you can make an insurance claim. If your passport is stolen, report it to the Consulate or Embassy at once.

Customs and Entry Regulations *see* Arriving p.110

Disabled visitors

Rome, with its ancient monuments and rough terrain, is not very suitable for disabled visitors, especially those confined to wheelchairs. However, the Vatican Museums, Sistine Chapel and St Peter's are accessible by wheelchairs.

Travellers are strongly recommended to check their particular requirements when making hotel or restaurant reservations. There are toilets for the disabled at the two Rome airports, at Stazione Termini, and at St Peter's Square. *Michelin Red Guide Italia* indicates hotels and restaurants with facilities for disabled visitors.

In Britain, RADAR, at 12 City Forum, 250 City Road, London EC1V 8AF ☎ 0171 250 3222 publishes factsheets and accommodation for the disabled traveller.

Driving

Driving in Rome requires nerves of steel, and can be a formidable experience which is best left to the experts. Romans blow their horns constantly, more to indicate their frustration – or merely their presence – than to alert other drivers to danger.

If you must drive through the capital, make sure that you

Horse and carriage.

are familiar with the rules of the road. Remember to drive on the right, and give way to traffic coming from the right.

Parking on the street is almost impossible in the city centre as many streets are limited to pedestrians, taxis and buses, or residents with permits. There are official car parks on the main routes into the city, but competition is fierce.

All the major routes into the city have frequent petrol stations; they are normally open from 7.30am-noon, and 4-7pm, but do vary , and depend on the season. Unleaded petrol is sold, but very few petrol stations accept credit cards, except on motorways. The following speed limits apply:

Cars

Motorways: 110kph/68mph (vehicles up to 1100cc); 130kph/80mph (over 1100cc)
Country roads: 90kph/56mph
Built-up areas: 50kph/31mph

Campers

Motorways: 100kph/62mph
Country roads: 80kph/50mph
Built-up areas: 50kph/31mph

Drivers should carry a full national or international driving licence, and an Italian translation of the licence unless it is a pink European licence; also insurance documents including a green card (no longer compulsory for EU members but strongly recommended), car registration papers, and nationality sticker for the rear of the car.

Headlight beams should be adjusted for right-hand drive, and a red warning triangle must be carried unless there are hazard warning lights on the car; you should also have a spare set of light bulbs. *See also* **Accidents and Breakdowns**

Electric Current

The voltage in Italy is usually 220V. Plugs and sockets are the round two-pinned ones, for which adaptors are generally required.

Embassies *see* Consulates

Emergencies

In an emergency, for
Ambulance or **Police** ☎ 113
Fire ☎ 115
Red Cross Ambulance ☎ 5510
Carabinieri ☎ 212121
City Police ☎ 67691
Automobile Club d'Italia
(car breakdown) ☎ 116
In cases of dire distress, the Consulate or Embassy may offer some help, but will not replace lost cash or plane tickets.

Etiquette

As in most places in the world, it is considered polite and respectful to cover up decently

Traffic police on duty.

in churches, museums, and theatres etc. Italians are a courteous people, and although less formal than many other Europeans, greet each other with 'good morning' (*buon giorno*) or 'good evening' (*buona sera*). This is usual when entering a restaurant, shop or hotel.

Excursions

Several coach companies and travel agencies organize tours of the city, or to places of interest outside the city such as the Catacombs, Ostia Antica and Tivoli. ATAC, at Piazza dei Cinquecento, run sightseeing bus tours, and the main coach tour companies with English-speaking guides are Carrani Tours, ☎ **474 2501**, Green Line Tours, ☎ **482 7480**, and CIT, ☎ **47941**. Details available from hotels or the tourist board (*see* **Tourist Information Offices**).

Guidebooks *see* Maps

Health

UK nationals should carry a Form E111 (forms available from post offices) which is produced by the Department of Health, and which entitles the holder to free urgent treatment for accident or illness in EU countries. The treatment will have to be paid

for in the first instance, but the money can be reclaimed later.

All foreign nationals are advised to take out comprehensive insurance cover, and to keep any bills, receipts and invoices to support any claim.

Lists of doctors can be obtained from hotels, chemists (*farmacia*) or police stations, and first aid and medical advice is also available at pharmacies (look out for the green or red cross).

Pharmacies are generally open from 9am-7.30pm, Monday to Saturday, with some variations, and lists of those which are open late or on Sundays are displayed at every chemist's shop. The Farmacia della Stazione, near Stazione Termini, is open 24 hours. First aid (*pronto soccorso*) with a doctor is also available at airports and railway stations.

Information *see* Tourist Information Offices

Language

Your efforts to speak Italian will be much appreciated everywhere, and even a few simple words and expressions are warmly received. On the next page there are a few words and phrases to help you make the most of your stay in Rome.

Yes/no Sì/no
Good morning Buon giorno [bwon jyorno]
Good afternoon/evening Buona sera [bwohna saira]
Please/thank you Per favore/grazie [pair favoray/gratsiay]
Do you speak English? Parla inglese? [parla inglaysay?]
How much is it? Quanto costa questo? [kwanto costa kwaisto?]
The bill, please Il conto, per favore [eel conto, pair favoray]
Excuse me Mi scusi [mee scoozi]
I'd like a stamp Vorrei un francobollo [vóray oon francobollo]
Do you accept travellers' cheques? Accetta travellers' cheques?
   [achetta…]
I don't understand Non capisco [nown capisko]

Laundry

There are no self-service launderettes in Rome, but if you leave your washing at a laundry you will be told when to collect it. Otherwise ask at your hotel or *pensione*, which may offer a laundry service for guests.

Lost Property

Report any loss or theft to the police at the *Questura*, Via San Vitale 15; ☎ **4686**. The central lost property office – Ufficio Oggetti Rinvenuti – is located at Via Niccolo Bettoni 1; ☎ **581 6040**. Airports and major railway stations have their own lost property offices, and if something goes missing in your hotel, check with the front desk and hotel security.

Should you lose any travel documents, contact the police, and in the event of a passport going missing, inform your Embassy or Consulate immediately (*see* **Consulates**). Lost or stolen travellers' cheques and credit cards should be reported immediately to the issuing company with a list of numbers, and the police should also be informed.

Maps

A full range of maps and guides is published by Michelin. Road Maps 988 *Italy* and 430 *Central Italy* will help you plan your routes when travelling through Italy.

   The *Michelin Green Guide Rome* contains detailed information on what to see and where to go in Rome. The

Green Guide Italy includes excellent information for all of Italy, including Rome. Information on restaurants and accommodation can be found in the *Michelin Red Guide Italia*.

Michelin on the Net:
www.michelin-travel.com
Our route-planning service covers all of Europe. Options allowing you to choose a preferred route are updated three times weekly, integrating on-going road-works, etc. Descriptions include distances and travelling times between towns, selected hotels and restaurants.

Money
The monetary unit of Italy is the Italian lira, and notes are issued in denominations of 1 000, 2 000, 5 000, 10 000, 20 000, 50 000 and 100 000 lire. Coins are of 5, 10, 20, 50, 100, 200 and 500 lire. All major credit cards, travellers' cheques and Eurocheques are accepted in most shops, restaurants, hotels, and some large motorway petrol stations.

There are no restrictions on the amount of currency visitors can take into Italy, but perhaps the safest way to carry large amounts of money is in travellers' cheques, which are widely accepted and exchanged. Exchange offices (*cambio*) are found at airports, terminals and larger railway stations, and at banks (*see also* **Banks**).

Try not to pay your hotel bill in foreign currency or travellers' cheques as the exchange rate is unlikely to be to your advantage.

Newspapers
Foreign newspapers and magazines can be bought all over the city from newsagents and kiosks. They are not cheap, especially the heavy Sunday papers. Besides the many Italian and Roman

Time to catch up on the news.

newspapers, the Catholic *L'osservatore Romano* prints a weekly edition in English.

Listings are published in *Wanted in Rome*, a free English-language newsletter which is distributed in bars, restaurants and newsagents, and comes out every fortnight.

Opening Hours

Shops are normally open from 8.30/9am-1pm, and from 3.30/4pm-7.30/8pm. Many shops close all day on Sunday and Monday morning.

Banks are open from 8.30am-1.30pm and often from 3-4pm.

Museums and galleries are mainly closed on Sunday afternoon and all day Monday. They are usually open from 9am-1/2pm, and sometimes from 5-8pm.

Post offices open 8.30am-2pm, Monday to Friday and 8.30-noon on Saturdays.

Churches open at about 7am–noon, and from 2-7pm. Main churches are open all day.

Photography

Good-quality film and camera equipment are readily available but expensive in Rome, and there are facilities for fast processing throughout the city. Before taking photographs in museums and art galleries it would be wise to check with staff as photography is usually restricted in these places.

Police

The *carabinieri* deal with serious crime in the city (☎ 212121); the *polizia* handle general crime, including lost passports and theft reports for insurance claims (☎ 67691).

A special police information office where tourists may get assistance is available on ☎ **4686**, ext **2102** or **2876**. Stolen or lost property may be reported here.

Post Offices

The main post office in Rome is in Piazza San Silvestro and, along with the post offices at Termini station and Leonardo da Vinci Airport, is open 8am-9pm, Monday to Friday, and 8am-12 noon on Saturday. It provides a 24-hour international telephone service, fax and telex, as well as *poste restante* facilities (letters should be addressed to the surname (underlined), c/o Palazzo delle Poste, Roma, Fermo Posta). Passports are required to collect *poste restante* mail.

Stamps (*francobolli*) are sold only by post offices, and tobacconists displaying a black and white 'T' sign. The Vatican City has its own stamps and postmarks, and its own post office. Letters posted in the special blue post boxes within the Vatican City must have Vatican stamps affixed, and they tend to arrive more quickly than those posted in ordinary Italian boxes.

Public Holidays

New Year's Day: 1 January
Epiphany: 6 January
Easter Sunday and Monday
Founding of Rome: 21 April
Liberation Day: 25 April
Labour Day: 1 May
Assumption Day: 15 August
All Saints: 1 November
Immaculate Conception: 8
   December
Christmas Day and Boxing
   Day: 25 and 26 December

Religion

Catholic: There are four Irish Catholic churches in Rome, and two others for English speakers. The main ones are San Silvestro, Piazza San Silvestro, ☎ 679 7775; and San Clemente, Via di San Giovanni in Laterno 45–7, ☎ 731 5723.
Anglican: All Saints, Via del Babuino 153, Piazza del Spagna; ☎ 679 4357.
Scottish Presbyterian: St Andrew's, Via XX Settembre 7; ☎ 482 7627.
Methodist: Piazza Ponte Sant'Angelo, ☎ 656 8314.
Jewish: Lungotevere dei Cenci 9, ☎ 686 4648.
Muslim: Viale della Moschea, ☎ 808 2167.

Colourful flowers brighten up the balconies above the streets.

Smoking

Smoking is banned in churches, museums and art galleries, and is discouraged in restaurants. There are separate non-smoking compartments in trains. Tobacconists (*tabacchi*), which carry a sign with a white 'T' inside a black rectangle, sell the major international brands of cigarettes.

Telephones

Italy is very well off for public telephones, which take either telephone cards to the value of 5 000, 10 000 and 15 000 lire, sold at newsagents and tobacconists, or 100, 200 and 500 lire coins; some older ones take telephone tokens (*gettoni*).

To telephone Rome from elsewhere in Italy dial 06 plus number, and to telephone elsewhere in Italy from Rome, dial the regional code plus number.

To make an international call from Italy, dial **00 61** for Australia, **001** for US and Canada, **00 44** for UK, and **00 64** for New Zealand. Cheap rates apply between 10pm-8am, Monday to Saturday, and all day Sunday.

International calls can be made from the orange call boxes dotted around the city, or from the Telephone Offices (*Telefoni*).

Time Difference

Italian standard time is GMT plus one hour. Italian summer time begins on the last weekend in March when the clocks go forward an hour (the same day as British Summer Time), and ends on the last weekend in September when the clocks go back (one month before BST ends).

Tipping

A service charge of 10 or 15 per cent is usually included in the bill at hotels and restaurants in Italy, but a tip (minimum amount 1000 lire) is also given where the service has been particularly pleasing. Check the bill to see if service has been included.

Usherettes who show you to your seat in a theatre should receive a tip, as well as hotel porters, airport and railway porters, and lavatory attendants. Taxi drivers will expect about 10 per cent.

Toilets

There are public conveniences at railway stations, airports and some museums, but otherwise they are quite rare. Use the toilets in bars and restaurants which, if not communal, are marked *signore* (women) and *signori* or *uomini* (men).

Tourist Information Offices

The Italian State Tourist Board (ENIT) is a good source of information and the three offices in Rome are staffed by English speakers (as well as speakers of other foreign languages). They have information on timetables, accommodation and programmes. The main office is at Via Margera 2, ☎ 49711. The Rome Provincial Tourist Board (EPT) has offices at Via Parigi 11, ☎ 488 1851; Stazione Termini, ☎ 487 1270; and Via Parigi 5, ☎ 488 3748. From these you can get hotel lists, brochures and free maps.

ENIT has offices in many countries, including the following English-speaking ones:

Australia and New Zealand: ENIT, c/o Alitalia, Orient Overseas Building, Suite 202, 32 Bridge Street, Sydney, NSW 2000; ☎ 2 92 471 308.
Canada: 1 Place Ville-Marie, Suite 1914, Montreal, Quebec H3B 2C3;
☎ 514 866 7667.
UK: 1 Princes Street, London W1R 8AY; ☎ 0171 408 1254.
USA: 630 Fifth Avenue, Suite 1565, New York, NY 10111;
☎ 212 245 4822.

Tours see Excursions

Transport

The best way to see the city is on foot, or by bus or tram. Remember, however, Roman traffic takes little if any notice of pedestrians, and crossing busy roads can be daunting for the inexperienced.

For travelling on public transport it is best to buy a plan of the city transport system. These are on sale in bookshops, newspaper kiosks, or at the information desk of ATAC, the main bus terminal at Piazza dei Cinquecento.

Bus tickets can be bought in advance at booths at the bus terminal, or at tobacconists, bars and newspaper kiosks. They should be stamped by a machine on boarding the bus. On-the-spot fines are imposed if you are caught without a validated ticket.

Integrated tickets for unlimited travel during one day, and weekly tourist tickets, are a good bargain, and can be bought from ATAC. There is also a night service.

A limited underground system runs through Rome on just two lines, but none of the stops is particularly close to tourist attractions. To see places of interest outside Rome, it is necessary either to hire a car or to go on one of the many coach trips.

Taxis can generally be found in special taxi ranks at railway stations and in the main parts of the city. They can also be called by telephone ☎ **3570**, **3875**, and **4995**. Fares are displayed on the meters, and there are extra charges for night service, Sundays and public holidays, luggage, and journeys outside town. Make sure the meter is started when you begin your journey, to avoid haggling over the fare when you arrive.

TV and Radio
Vatican Radio broadcasts English-language religious news programmes. During the tourist season, the Italian state radio and television network (RAI) broadcasts news in English on the radio at 10am, Monday to Saturday, and at 9.30am on Sunday. RAI television broadcasts only in Italian. Many short-wave radios pick up the BBC World Service in English.

Vaccinations see Before You Go p.110

Water
Rome's water is safe to drink, unless the tap has a sign saying *acqua non potabile* (not for drinking). It is usual to order a bottle of water (*acqua minerale*) with meals.

Youth Hostels see Accommodation

Dining al fresco on Via Vittorio Veneto.

INDEX

This index includes entries
for place names in both
English (where used in the
guide) and in Italian (*italics*).

INDEX